Encounter with Power

Encounter with Power

A Journey from the Toltec Perspective

Jessica Rzeszewski

Order this book online at www.trafford.com
or email orders@trafford.com

Most Trafford titles are also available at major online book retailers.

© Copyright 2007, 2013 Jessica Rzeszewski.

All rights reserved. No part of this publication may be reproduced, stored in a retrieval system, or transmitted, in any form or by any means, electronic, mechanical, photocopying, recording, or otherwise, without the written prior permission of the author.

Printed in the United States of America.

ISBN: 978-1-4251-3070-1 (sc)
ISBN: 978-1-4907-1683-1 (e)

Because of the dynamic nature of the Internet, any web addresses or links contained in this book may have changed since publication and may no longer be valid. The views expressed in this work are solely those of the author and do not necessarily reflect the views of the publisher, and the publisher hereby disclaims any responsibility for them.

Any people depicted in stock imagery provided by Thinkstock are models, and such images are being used for illustrative purposes only.
Certain stock imagery © Thinkstock.

Trafford rev. 10/11/2013

Trafford
PUBLISHING   www.trafford.com

North America & international
toll-free: 1 888 232 4444 (USA & Canada)
fax: 812 355 4082

Dedication

To Carlos Castaneda whose writings and dreaming together ushered me into the world of perception and power.

Preface

The Toltec Path is about action; it is not about words at all. But words are the springboard from which action can take place thus this book was conceived. While writing *Encounter with Power: A Journey from the Toltec Perspective*, it was not my intent to make it a workbook, but Power stepped in and suggested that a third element was necessary as an addition to the concepts and stories presented. That third element was an action plan in the form of questions and practical steps with which the reader can choose to engage. The book offers a powerful triad: cognition (or in this context, words which describe experience), feelings (our stories formed of a backbone in feelings), and action (a game plan for change). If any element of the triad is missing, change is not likely to take place and without change we remain exactly as we are at this moment. And my guess is that you picked up this book as a means to entertain, organize, challenge, or educate yourself—in other words, to move from where you are at this moment to somewhere else. In this desire for change you are available for exploration and growth. Whatever the reason for picking up the book, the change you seek will occur by involving yourself in all three elements of the triad above.

It is in the nature of Power to place us at a threshold for change; it is in our nature to either embrace or to deny that change. It is within our Power to decide. What better way to take action than with exercise?

Read over the questions and practical steps at the end of each chapter and allow your eye to choose which ones will most impact you upon answering and engaging with them. The eyes are an entryway into our souls and they have the ability to decide how we might best proceed—allow them to do what they are best at doing! If one or all of the questions "catch your eye" then proceed to answer them. By answering the questions or doing the exercise you will be taking the necessary steps towards change through the triad mentioned above. I have provided you with the information and the stories and you will be taking action in order to make the information your own. You will be translating information into knowledge. I trust that Power will proceed in accordance to its natural bent, meaning that if given the opportunity, Power will transform you! To that end, I wish you well.

Table of Contents

Introduction xi
1. Power Is.. 1
2. The Enemy 22
3. Accessible To Power 41
4. A Different Language 57
5. Power Plants 71
6. Manifesting Power 89
7. The Hunt for Power 104
8. The Power in Dreaming 116
9. A Waste of Power 133
10. Tale of Power 147

Introduction

Power is indispensable for anyone traveling along the Toltec Path. A warrior/sorcerer in the Toltec tradition knows that power will reveal itself sooner or later. On this journey, the warrior/sorcerer travels into the heart of power itself. Power, in all of its manifestations, is where the warrior/sorcerer gains the necessary energy to walk the Toltec path. Power does so because its appearance is an immutable Toltec law. At the very same time that power is the warrior/sorcerer's lifeblood, power is also an enemy that must be challenged, confronted, and subdued in order to move along the path with any degree of success. If the warrior/sorcerer succumbs to the allure of power she is incapacitated and might as well hang up her weapons to the victor. This vexing dilemma faces every warrior/sorcerer at some crossroad in her journey. At first it is unfathomable that something so vital can also be so deadly.

How can power be one and the same thing? It is a mystery that must be unraveled or it becomes a veritable barricade to growth. Either the warrior/sorcerer learns to handle power or she is crushed to bits by a force that rolls over her without conscience. It is an act of absolute certainty: unless the warrior/sorcerer engages in deadly battle with power, she will be powerless to proceed. This book is about how a traveler, a warrior/sorcerer following the Toltec path, engages with power from the initial tentative step of entering foreign land without direction, to moving deep into the interior of Toltec country as a seasoned traveler. There is no other way. Power is the topography.

This topic is not new but neither has it been approached with focus placed entirely on power itself. This introductory study is aimed at looking at that illusive yet pervasive force which is all encompassing to the sojourner on this path. The entirety of the Toltec precepts would cover volumes, and rightfully so. A discipline of this magnitude takes years to fathom, not unlike following any number of paths that demand a follower's all. Because a warrior/sorcerer engages power from the first moment of her involvement, she continues her engagement with power through to the end, and there is a need to identify and clarify the pulse, the heartbeat, the flow, found in its very essence. This book will serve that need as a magnifying glass serves the need of the scientist; it will give a close-up look in order to study what the naked eye cannot see alone. Power is to the warrior/sorcerer what blood is to the body; without it neither the warrior/sorcerer nor the body could exist.

A caveat about language needs to be addressed before we go on. It involves the term "Toltec." My choice was to refer to the syntax of sorcery as either "Toltec" or sorcery. Either term is suitable for our purposes. Our goal is to examine "power" as though through a microscope and to look at it in minute detail for an extended period of time. In the process of discussing power, I needed an umbrella term that would refer to the specific act of moving perception beyond our accustomed manner of perceiving, but also a term that would encompass the broader system of actions that describe what a warrior/sorcerer does. "Toltec", as I am using it, includes the history of sorcery from millennia past in conjunction with the popular usage of sorcery as a path to follow today. I am using the term in a global sense. I am primarily interested in passing on knowledge about a lifestyle, not in defining specific parameters or declaring heritage as a Toltec. The term is used as a frame of reference and not as a title of designation. Please take it in that vein.

Every attempt has been made to use common language that those reading will be able to grasp without having an in-depth background in Toltec terminology. I remember well when I first began reading literature

Introduction

regarding the Toltec path and feeling a sense of frustration at terminology that seemed to keep the reader from gaining any foothold at all into what was being transmitted! Certain terms are not in the category of "user friendly" until the reader grasps on tight like a bulldog onto a bone and begins to experience the action that the words convey for her self. There is also a general assumption that if you have picked up this book, there has been previous interest and association with Toltec principles and therefore you won't be totally in the dark when more common terms are used. There is a sense of irony in attempting usage of any language in describing and explaining what power is and what power does. Power is elusive and can easily defy being put into the linear format that writing entails but words do a good enough job to get us started.

It is in the nature of the path to have an inimical relationship with things that occur in our minds. The artificial mind has operated during a large period of our existence and is more often than not the source of our words. Grappling with the words and the concepts being described by the words are two very different things. The goal here is to use language that doesn't impede the concepts being shared. It is difficult enough to grasp the underlying spirit of which the words are poor symbols from the beginning. Language springs from the human capacity to communicate with words yet words can too easily be placed as proxy for experience. This path is based on action but words come as close as they possibly can; they mimic the act, and thereby become handy tools for transferring the concepts. Let the words fall over you as though you are standing in a shower feeling the water droplets touch you ceaselessly. Some of the words will impact; they will impact because they carry enough force and you are standing in the direct path of descent. Others will fall by the wayside, thus they were not intended to influence. Let them go. They will serve their purpose at a different time and place on your journey if need be.

Here then is where we are headed. First, it is critical to delve into the word itself: Power. The word is loaded with meaning, and in many ways we must strip it of its meaning or else we will be grossly misled from the outset. The word needs definition within the context of the art of sorcery in order not to intermingle with the context of the word as it is normally used.

Second, we'll look at power as an enemy. Couldn't a less offensive word be used? We'll discover why that value-laden word leaves us little choice. A word with any less force would do our study an injustice. The term puts the warrior/sorcerer into a stance that can only be held if the object facing us is an archenemy.

Third, accessibility to power comes differently depending on where we are on the path. As we access power we change in a myriad of ways at first imperceptible. As we move along in our growth we discover that power changes, too. It is all a mystery at first until we are able to deftly draw the sword and wield it in one swift and deadly arc of victory that gives us the gain we are seeking. Knowing how and where power comes will inform us as to how and where we need to be in order to meet it successfully.

Fourth, power speaks to us: the language of omens. Communication occurs between the warrior/sorcerer and power but it is not in the manner we may be most familiar with. We must begin to "speak" without words, using all of our senses to engage in battle. This mode of communication is a primary conduit through which power travels.

Fifth, we begin to objectify power and find it in all kinds of places and things that reach out to us because of the power imbued therein, such as objects with a sentient nature. These power plants have a checkered history for those seeking power so they bear close examination. Not everyone engages with them, yet power plants have much to offer.

Sixth, we begin to manifest power. In other words, a vital shift takes place as to where we place our attention. From that vantage point we begin to see power in all of its manifestations. Funny, we'd not noticed before!

Seventh, hunts for power begin; we actively search for power whether in places, objects, times, or people. We become aware that power is everywhere, even in places we'd not ever noticed before. We become attuned to finding out how to engage with it in the weirdest places.

Introduction

Eighth, our dreaming changes. Slowly or suddenly, depending on our bent, we begin to manifest power through our dreaming. Dreaming is our only long-term source of power although we have been raised to believe that dreaming is illusory to our everyday living. We soon discover that dreaming is exactly the opposite: the source of power itself and that this dreaming is occurring in our daily waking life.

Ninth, we realize that all of our hard earned power can be used carelessly and cheaply. Tracking our wanton use we begin to conserve and hoard, not desiring to squander this magical elixir.

Last, we have tales of power to tell. Our stories tell about our journey, even catapulting us beyond their telling, into the mystery that is sorcery.

Each chapter is opened with a story on Dreaming, or those experiences that occur in a reality apart from everyday life. Pay attention to how the stories change as we advance through the reading. They show a progression to the art and practice of sorcery in that greater and greater awareness is gained as the skills discussed are exercised. In light of that, each chapter is also closed with a story on Tracking. They also have a progression to them as the warrior/sorcerer develops this art that is the twin of Dreaming.

Ah, the spirit of sorcery is power! How very simple! How very deceptive! Power is our source of sustenance and our lethal enemy, yet we cannot serve two masters. The crux of the matter for the warrior/sorcerer is that she will make power one or the other. If this were an easy, black and white choice, we wouldn't need any further elaboration. Power is not so easily deciphered!

Finally, we have taken of the wellspring of life; power resides within and we command it at will. We have come so very far into the heartland of this Toltec land! Power is a gift. We partake of it as such, a gift that is ours to unfold and to discover its untold wealth. How we use it will be our tale of power!

1.

Power Is

Apple was crouched ready to pounce. Her body was low and lean along the carpet as I sat and watched from the couch. She was walking stealthily in front of the rocking chair even though nothing was to be seen out of the ordinary. Eyes scanning the area in front of her, she looked as though only she could see the invisible mouse right in front of her nose. Spooked, I sat up on the couch and leaned forward. I hadn't been feeling well the last three days; in fact the flu had left me feeling lousy and feverish. Problem was I was not convinced as to the real origin of the illness: spirit or viral? My head was heavy and congested, my heart was clouded and hanging low within. For months my internal interrogator relentlessly questioned and doubted my every move. It was not enough emotionally to have separated from my husband of twenty years in the past six months, but at the same time I had begun to delve into some crazy system of sorcery popularized by Carlos Castaneda nearly forty years before. The really crazy thing about it was that what he said made perfect sense to me, at least while reading. But at the moment, I was light headed and exhausted from coughing incessantly and watching with fascination as my cat was stalking the living room, cautious, almost paranoid as if hunting something in the ether I could not see.

Who wants to be bothered with the definition of a word? Grab a dictionary and be done with it. But the two initial words we are working with as we get started are much too volatile. Words get heavier with use and these two words have been used for a long time in two separate worlds: daily reality and the sorcerer's realm. Let's tease them out from those separate realities. One of the reasons to do that is because as a warrior/sorcerer (two more words to be defined a bit later) the use of these two terms will determine our movement on the path. No kidding! Say you are seated across the table from someone you know. They lean over the table while gazing into your eyes to whisper slowly, "I love you." There are a dozen ways to respond. Each and every response will be impacted by your definition of that phrase and their definition of it and the history between you and the day before and the night to come. How you define "love" will impact what happens from the moment you respond to the spoken words. The word "love" has become a verbal and visual meme that has seasoned over the centuries and now wears a thousand faces. "Power" and "enemy" bear the same weight as far as being terms with loaded histories.

A second reason to define them fully and carefully from the outset is that they are used in two different syntaxes. One is the syntax of our common world. The second is the syntax of the warrior/sorcerer. If we understand from the very beginning that these two words are rich and pregnant in both realms we will have less confusion about their use. Primarily we will be speaking in the context of the realm of sorcery, a landscape less familiar to many than that of the everyday world. Overlapping terms is a common occurrence as we attempt to speak from both realms, but it is also the source of a lack in clarity when the words are specific to each realm. Defining our terms carefully, clearing them of weighty confusion, will lessen the possibility of becoming muddled and hazy later on.

The adjectives used thus far to describe power leave the reader with a tease of what the word power means but not a clear definition. Already we have spoken of power as indispensable, lifeblood, an enemy, and a force. Exactly what is "power" for the warrior/sorcerer? What is the definition for the term that becomes the driving force for this book and the impetus for writing the book in the first place?

Power is a force that provides the warrior/sorcerer with the energy she needs, to be all that she has the capacity to be, in a universe that is infinite, for the express purpose of gaining freedom, or a state of perceptual openness. While the definition is abstract at this point in time, it may be the best we can provide. Initially, sorcery terms appear abstract. They are difficult to grasp because they are outside of our prevalent usage; in fact, they can be so far from our accustomed manner of thinking as to be another way of thinking altogether. This inexperience with sorcery terms can initially elicit a lack of comprehension. At the same time, part of the difficulty in giving a definition to the term is that the definition can change depending on our experience.

Many examples are given in order to get a sense of terms that can at first sound abstract and, therefore, foreign. A visual metaphor might be helpful, too. Power is the rocket that will propel us into the wonder, mystery, and vastness of outer space. In the vastness of outer space we will find freedom. And, freedom is the absence of all that we do, think, and say that inhibits us from experiencing the potential of our capability as perceiving beings. Throughout the book, we will explore many facets of power that will contribute to a comprehensive understanding of the term by the end of our study.

My first known experience with Power came at a sweat lodge, although I didn't see it coming ahead of time. At the end of the third round inside the lodge saturated with heat, the temperature became excruciating. I was exhausted to the point that I lay on the ground fighting within myself. Do I speak aloud and ask to have the flap opened to allow in cool air, or do I continue to breathe through the sage and hang tight? I quieted the chatter inside my mind and lay still, unaware of others around me. Time stopped.

When I focused my awareness on my surroundings again, I noticed that most of the forty odd people were no longer inside the lodge. I became aware of two people lying prone; they were quiet and did not seem to be aware of me. I crawled over to them. There was something of imminent importance to tell each one. Without any inhibition whatsoever, I lay on top of each one in turn, whispering the knowledge to each in their ear. With astounding clarity I spoke to them of their heart's most urgent concern. I then crawled over to the lodge entrance. Moments later, the woman crawled past me as she was leaving the lodge while I was in a quandary as to whether or not to mention anything about her abortion. Time was irrelevant; I didn't know if the abortion was a past or future event.

There was no thinking, per se, but I began to be aware that the "thoughts" inside my head were not familiar to my everyday thinking. I seated myself at the entrance to the lodge. People were outside, milling around the fire pit, washing off the mud caked on their bodies from inside the lodge, chatting, and generally unaware of me seated in the twilight. The evening was approaching. I was reveling in being seated peacefully, feeling the coolness of the coming evening, and gazing at everyone who was around me. My gaze soon shifted to the altar directly in front of me. Staring at the dozens of objects placed on the mound, I was blissfully at peace as I gazed at them one after another.

Soon people came within arms length of me, asking if I was going to change out of my soaked clothes before joining everyone for the evening meal. But I wasn't the least bit interested in food or clothing. I was immersed in knowledge! Anyone coming within a foot or two of me was game; I could read their precise thoughts. I knew things I couldn't have possibly known. I had never met these people before this evening! Calling out to the sweat leader, I asked that he gather everyone together because I had something to tell everyone. The sweat leader noticed my shouting, difficult not to in the small encampment, and rushed over, quickly motioning the fire tenders to attend to me.

The sweat leader was interested in getting me back into my body. I was more interested in the knowledge that was unfolding before me like pearls of wisdom. My body felt like a foreign thing I had no awareness of at the moment. More than thoughts—the knowledge was the very essence of whomever and whatever I focused my awareness onto. I would look at someone and instantly know the core of that person. I even turned the spotlight of inquisition onto myself. Questions I had about childhood, marriage, psychoanalytic training, who and what I was, all came speeding toward me, a freight train of pure, unadulterated knowledge. I was immersed in a wonderland of power that knew no bounds. It was a power brand new to me, never experienced before, and I reveled in it for days afterwards. Power was now within my conscious awareness. I would never view it in the same way as before.

We will learn to interact equally with Power as a verb and as a noun. Of course you noticed the capital "P" when the term was used in the last sentence. Power in the sorcery realm is a quality, a force, a feeling of such magnitude that it influences everything we do. It cannot be claimed to have the same preeminence in the daily world. It is also sentient and therefore commanding of our respect, thus throughout the text it will be honored as such. As a verb and as a noun it operates as a dynamic duo. The art of the warrior/sorcerer is to differentiate when Power is acting on her and when she herself can take Power and use it to act either in the daily world of waking or in the sorcery realm.

It is unfortunate that in today's world primary aspects of Toltec functioning are too easily defined in the sphere of a common world mindset. An example is the manner in which Toltec precepts are often "psychologized" or made to be about the mind and motives of human beings interacting and living amongst other human beings. By being presented in this way Toltec precepts run the risk of losing their potency. Power is one of them. If we only speak of Power as a quality, force, or feeling familiar to us in the daily world in which we live, we miss entirely that it is a primary foundation piece of Toltec livelihood and well-being. Power is our distinct heritage as warrior/sorcerers but only after we have battled, claimed, and commanded it.

Power as viewed in the world's eye is often for the few rather than the many. It is status and sway. Used in any area of influence including socio-political, environmental, relational, or spiritual, power is a quality that is defined by how much, how strong, and how quick it is wielded. The reputation for its abuse is legion. Power drives the mass of humanity whether they perceive of themselves as possessing it or not. Power has a nasty reputation on the surface of the planet; it is the conqueror, the despot that will win at any costs. We have personified power to be a Machiavellian character of untold evil and influence. Power has a reputation that, if taken as accurate, will cripple the warrior/sorcerer from engaging with it fully.

Then there are those who know that power used in that manner is evidence of the abuse of power, not its proper use. But wherein lays the dividing line? There are those who wield power with jurisdiction that is prudent and proper, and to those who do they have an inkling of Power from the realm of sorcery. Many disciplines claiming intimacy with Power have indeed tapped into the source itself. Many of those reading may have put their endeavors into any number of disciplines including martial arts, metaphysical systems, spiritual belief systems, and even, dietary systems. There are many belief systems that empower the practitioner to a lifestyle that produces growth and evolution. I have practiced half a dozen of them, including religion, shamanism, and psychology. It is the act of sorcery, however, the wielding of perception through the medium of Power that puts the warrior/sorcerer into direct contact with Power without a social context for definition.

Toltec acts have become generalized in the everyday world. These acts have become look-alike behavior that has become popularized within the context of a social matrix. For example, the Toltec term "recapitulation" has been twinned with "processing emotional baggage." "Tracking" has become twinned with "assessment and introspection" and a "petty tyrant" is aligned with an "emotional abuser". In an effort to cross over concepts, one syntax to another, it has been convenient to make use of terms or phrases that match the meaning as close as possible in the realm of language. This gets the practitioner onto the playing field, but doesn't mean he's standing at the bat and making contact with the ball. Power is to be used in the context and syntax of sorcery and for the warrior/sorcerer that can only be defined in the face of Power itself. This book is about one warrior/sorcerer interacting with Power, telling a tale of Power. All tales of Power are unique to the individual warrior/sorcerer as are each and every precept on the path. At the same time, there are identifying and directional markers that can show the way.

The ultimate goal of the path is freedom and Power is present throughout the journey, but it is the warrior/sorcerer's ability to discern how Power is evidenced that makes all the difference in the world as to how her journey unfolds. At first the idea that there is a force that is vital to sustenance but that is deadly to mess with seems incongruent. How can there be a force, a quality, an essence that I can't live with, but neither can I live without? It doesn't make sense, and therein may be a warrior/sorcerers' first error. Nothing makes sense in a world unfamiliar to us. Trying to make sense of the world can lead the warrior/sorcerer down a rabbit trail she may never return from. Haven't we done that for way too long as it is—added meaning to everything about our lives so that there is no longer any mystery? It is too easy to try to understand, to try to comprehend the world, and by doing so, to miss the mystery therein.

The trick is not to make any sense of it; making sense of something only lends it familiarity, and therefore contempt. Once we think we know what is going on, once we become familiar with a person, an idea, or a system, we have a tendency to lose our objectivity toward it, or to treat that object with less wonder and openness because we have concluded something about it. In other words, we have defined the person, idea, or system and that very familiarity, that knowing of the object, lends itself to judgments or contempt. The trick is to experience the world, to feel the world in its entire sentience, rather than to try and make sense of it in order to understand what is happening.

Power is invisible, yet it is not. Power is a feeling, yet it is not. Power is an object, yet it is not. Power is a force, yet it is not. Power is energy and all the warrior/sorcerer cares about in the end is how she handles energy. There are other sources of energy in the warrior/sorcerer realm, intent being one of them, but for this study Power is the focus. It is tempting to use metaphor to describe Power. "Sounds like electricity to me. Use it correctly and you won't get hurt; use it without an appropriate channel and you can get fried!" But metaphor as a tool can be stretched only so far, and we're talking about a living, conscious, moving energy that cannot be easily quantified into a metaphor. To be known Power must be experienced!

What is the danger in using the word as society does? On the surface it looks like none. But a quick delineation between the world and the sorcerer's realm will help to push through the surface in order not to be trapped skating on thin ice as we move through the discussion. A sorcerer's paradox is stated first. Much like a koan, the statement evokes mystery and perhaps even confusion due to its lack of familiarity and usage: "the world" and "the sorcerer's realm" is the same thing! And much like a koan, the full comprehension of that statement takes the development and maturity of the warrior/sorcerer in order to unravel.

I state it because so much in the sorcerer's realm requires that the warrior/sorcerer grapple with paradoxes and mysteries and koans as a means of movement along the path. If the two terms, "the world" and "the sorcerer's realm" are differentiated too stringently from the outset the warrior/sorcerer will lose the fluidity necessary to maintain any movement along the path. I mention it here as an ongoing paradox, of which there are many for a warrior/sorcerer to unravel because it's an activity that is never ending and ever expedient. Power is a koan that needs unraveling before the warrior/sorcerer transcends its mystery.

The present discussion is a difficult one to grasp particularly if Power has not been experienced before but as the warrior/sorcerer travels she becomes aware that Power comes within the circumstances at hand that best pertain to her. My experience with the sweat lodge is a prime example. I experienced Power at a rate that was most suited to me individually. You will do the same. The warrior/sorcerer will grasp the amount and the depth of knowledge that she is ready for, and at exactly the time that is most opportune. The skill in being able to know beyond a shadow of doubt and to act from that knowing is what defines the position of the warrior/sorcerer in whatever abode she finds herself in, including the nebulous boundaries that evolve between the daily world she sees or the mysterious sorcerer's realm that can so easily elude her.

Apple stalked the living room because she could sense something present at the time that I could not. I recognized her movements as odd in that I'd never observed her acting so strangely before, but I could not decipher anything about the object that had so skillfully trapped her attention. Power was present but was not within my frame of reference to "decode." It wasn't long before I could, and oddly enough, the experience involved another cat.

Early one morning I awoke to feel a cat at the top of the bed, carefully placing its paws on the bed sheets. Funny—I awoke, did not open my eyes, but knew beyond a shadow of a doubt that the pressure I sensed was from a cat. I did not stop to ponder how I knew what I knew. Instantly, I was riveted by the weight of the cat's paws as she deliberately placed one paw after the other, as though mesmerized by her own simplicity. I was mesmerized. How could she move with such precision? She was fastidiously placing each paw as though once placed it would be held forever in that spot. Slowly, my mind entered the scene.

"Wait! Apple is outside for the night. Who let her inside the house? How can there possibly be a cat walking along the top of the mattress near my pillow? Has Laurelle left for swim practice yet? Maybe she opened the door for Apple to come in at 5:30 this morning. Wait just a minute! Open your eyes! If you open your eyes, you will be able to determine if the cat walking along your bed is Apple."

I struggled to lift my eyelids from off their pupils. Had it ever been so difficult to open my eyes? My eyelids weighed a ton. I turned my head slightly, towards the head of the bed to see the cat that I could feel quite distinctly. One eye opened. There was the headboard, against which the mattress was abutted, with a fitted sheet covering it. There was nothing else: no cat, no paws, no Apple. I was alone in the room. What had just happened? It took me nearly two years and a dozen more feline appearances before I found out. You will find out more in the following chapters.

If the world as we know it is the same as the sorcerer's realm how then are we to differentiate it? Power in the world is experienced largely through three arenas: socio-political, financial/material, and psychological/spiritual. Yes, there is environmental Power but it cannot compete with the big three; if it could our planet would not be in the condition that she is in. Because the majority of humanity has defined environmental Power in terms of lesser significance when compared to the other arenas, environmental Power has become a passive entity provided temporary obeisance only when it explodes. A tsunami, earthquake, or flood of global impact usually gets our attention!

Despite the occasional natural disaster demanding attention, the three arenas of socio-political, financial/material, and psychological/spiritual dominate the world for most of mankind; albeit in varying degrees, these three have society's primary attention. Power is filtered through them because society has agreed these arenas hold colossal value. History has shown that these three areas appeal to humanity according to the variability of the time; therefore, it is there that our attention gets placed. The gradients as to preference may differ for each individual but they are, at the very least, observable.

The warrior/sorcerer, on the other hand, enters into a different syntax, an entirely new cognition, when entering Toltec territory. It is outside of anything she is consciously aware of even though it is precisely where she is headed. Using language as a metaphor it might be easy to equate the difference between the two by saying, "It's like learning a foreign language." But it involves more than becoming bi-lingual. It is placing oneself outside of time and space, thought and language, to develop and to rediscover knowledge that mankind no longer accesses on a regular basis. This act of paying attention requires the warrior/sorcerer's awareness and is developed as she encounters Power.

Mankind has left untapped much of his potential. Whether we acknowledge it or not, there is a vast field of knowledge that mankind has relegated to either the unknown or the unknowable. We cannot fathom being outside of all that we know and this tendency to not see what we don't know applies to Power as well. Power experienced inside of the big three paradigms is all that we know, therefore, we barely have thought, much less put into words, a description of anything different.

After my initial experience at the sweat lodge, the unknown occurred again one weekend while camping in that same small valley in the hills of Southern California. I was returning to my tent to gather my belongings together after a long day of involvement with people at the sweat lodge. I was several hours' drive from home and after such a long, hot day, I decided to pack up my things and drive home rather than to stay overnight. Don and Lynn had set up their tent next to mine the evening before. As I kneeled down at the front flap of my tent, I glanced over to see their shadows projected onto the tent from the glow of their kerosene lantern. I could hear them murmuring to each other softly; their voices were gentle and caring. I smiled. They were newly wed and had been intensely focused on each other the entire weekend. Grabbing my sleeping bag, I began to stuff it into its bag. Then pulling all of my scattered clothes toward me, I jammed them into the duffle bag. I was too tired to take the time to fold things in any kind of orderly manner. I pushed myself off my knees in order to stand up. It was time to throw things into the car. I glanced over at my neighbors once again.

Don and Lynn were not there! Not only were Don and Lynn not in their tent, but also there was no tent! The area immediately next to me was empty! I scanned the darkness around me. Where were they? How long had I taken to get my things gathered together? Not nearly long enough for two adults, a walk-in tent, and a weekend's worth of camping gear to disappear twenty feet from me.

Power exists outside of our minds, outside of time, outside of space! It relates not at all to this human world and therein is often our initial difficulty in even conceiving of it. But the warrior/sorcerer has inklings from the start and she begins to pursue what is initially a mystery. As the mystery unfurls the warrior/sorcerer becomes less and less surprised that Power is ever present, ever mindful, and available for taking if the warrior/sorcerer has the strength to do so. The element of surprise is in the following story, as is the mystery of the environment, and how the environment manifests the Power that the warrior/sorcerer seeks.

Early in my Toltec journey, I would go to the desert. I wanted to speak to the desert about what was happening in my life. This particular morning, I wanted to talk about Power. I understood intellectually what I was reading about Power, but what was happening in my life that signaled that Power was engaged with me? How would I know if it was? That—I couldn't pinpoint. My plan was to go hiking in Joshua Tree National Forest, located in the Southern California high desert. In the past, the desert would readily speak to me while I walked, telling me what I wanted to know, and this time was no different. I arrived the evening before and spent the night in a hotel. The desert is magic in the early morning and I wanted to be hiking well before the sun rose too high in the sky making hiking unbearable with its heat. I parked my car and oriented myself. Looking carefully in all four directions I gave myself visual markers on the horizon before I headed off, because soon my car, the road, and means of contact with anyone, would be far, far away.

Walking for hours, I watched and listened for anything and everything that crossed my path that would inform me about my query. Sometimes the voice of Spirit would come in the crows that flew over my head, or the cave that harbored me from the rising sun for a time, or the red tailed hawk that screeched as he circled hundreds of feet in the air above me, or the gargantuan boulders that I tried to scramble over and around. At one point, I paused and spoke aloud my intention to have contact with the world of Power that I was certain surrounded me. I presented myself to the unseen world of Power even though I was uncertain about the impact my actions would trigger. Hours later, as I began to take stock of what the desert had said, I walked slowly back to the side of the road where my car was parked.

As I crossed the road, a gentleman approached me. I hadn't seen him while I was on the other side of the road, had I? I glanced around to orient myself. Hiking the desert had put me in such a state of reverie that I was startled to see anyone, and even more startled to think about having a coherent conversation with anyone at the moment. I wanted to continue pondering what the desert had said and I was not the least bit interested in talking to a stranger. Where had he come from anyway? Was he with anyone? Did he want a ride from me? What did he want? There he stood, between my car and me. He looked directly at me, while mumbling something I couldn't quite decipher.

"Excuse me?" I approached him close enough to hear and speak, hoping that the tone in my voice would convey that I wasn't interested in idle chatter.

"What kind of power do you use?" he asked.

My mouth dropped open. How in the world did he know the reason I had trekked the desert all morning? That question was at the heart of what I'd been asking since dawn!

"What?" I stammered, unsure of how to answer this stranger, who kept smiling despite my obvious consternation. Did he know what he was asking me?

"What type of engine does your car have, rotary or cylinder?" He pointed to the hood of my car, as if doing so would clear up my confusion.

Even then, I wasn't sure how to answer. All I could fathom in the moment was the wonder of the desert: Power itself had employed this stranger to challenge me into answering my own question.

Thinking along about the difference in syntax used by the warrior/sorcerer, a question naturally arises at this point. After all, the stranger on the desert was talking about my car's engine, whereas I was talking about the world of sorcery. If Power to a warrior/sorcerer is impossible to define from the outset, and yet it is somewhat clear that Power as the world defines it is not what we are talking about, then how does the warrior/sorcerer even know what to look for and what to pursue? The question must be asked. Questions are a unique medium of exchange in the Toltec context, and precisely so because we are the only creatures that use words as a form of communication.

Even though questions beg for information, information is not necessarily what we need. An advertisement in *Times Magazine* declared: "We are drowning in information and starved for knowledge." Little did the author of that add know the statement is aligned squarely with Toltec thought! But questions, even though readily engendering information rather than knowledge, also channel our attention. The stranger on the desert was asking for information, whereas I was attending to something entirely different, and yet his question focused my attention. As a commodity of energy, attention is vital to growth because it leads to awareness. We are heading toward increasing knowledge, and awareness is the highway we want to be on.

Power is the fuel; attention is the vehicle we drive. Questions act as the steering wheel. The question of how the warrior/sorcerer even knows what to look for and what to pursue relevant to Power highlights the active agent that is Power. In other words, Power is a source that is active in hunting the warrior/sorcerer as equally as the warrior/sorcerer is hunting it. It is a costly mistake to only view the warrior/sorcerer as the one doing the looking, hunting, searching, stalking. Power is after us! That puts an entirely different spin on the situation than if we were the sole party on the move hunting a prey that does not expect us.

Knowing that Power is an indefinable, invisible force that is potentially dangerous we must be aware that it is far and above a simple cat and mouse chase. Instead our engagement is a reciprocal one that demands all of our available energy to even begin! Our opponent is after us and it is unclear yet as to why. Power is a powerful verb.

To answer our question then: Power will show itself and by doing so we will learn what to look for. Not only will we learn what Power is, but also we will learn how to use it. We will learn how Power shows itself, how it manifests, and what in the world we do with it once it is ours.

In defining what Power is, a term that is more easily describable by what it does than by what it is, there is a component of its "is-ness" that is wise to be aware of from the outset. Power is this: deceptive, alluring, and seductive. We have yet to take a look at Power as an enemy, that comes next, but it is all too easy to expect Power to be "monsterish" and something to abhor and to fend off. That reaction to Power is deceptive. If we continue to view Power from that perspective we'll open up the possibility of being broadsided and end up not having a clue as to what hit us. If the face of Power is initially unrecognizable, at the very least be aware that at its core Power is one of the most pleasurable and desirable of acquisitions. It will bewitch us with flattery and we'll never be the wiser for it! Being cognizant of the nature of Power contributes to knowing the enemy. Without knowing the enemy we have no chance of besting it.

Power is taking on big time status. In the world, big time status implies big time opposition. It is the same in the sorcerer's realm. An enemy is on our doorstep. Outlined by many a modern day Toltec author Power is one of four enemies to present themselves to the warrior/sorcerer. We've already stated that Power will show up in the life of the warrior/sorcerer at some point, but now is the time to reiterate that Power shows itself as a class one enemy.

Historically, a warrior/sorcerer has four great enemies: fear, clarity, power, and old age. Power not only shows up as an enemy but we must approach it as an enemy. The two are vastly different agendas and yet go hand in hand. The reciprocal relationship between Power and the warrior/sorcerer is best recognized rather than to foolishly think we are approaching a static barrier to be overcome by might and valor. No! Power is. Power is energy. Power is an enemy. Amidst all of the attempts at explaining and defining our term it is most critical to grasp these last two: Power is energy. Power is an enemy. It is vital to keep in mind that what concerns a warrior/sorcerer is her engagement and interaction with energy.

The universe is composed of energy: a state of being that quantum physics has "confirmed." We live in a holographic universe in which energy is never destroyed but reconfigures and realigns itself over and over. The warrior/sorcerer wants to be able to manipulate the energy she encounters through Power as a primary source for income and output of that universal energy. Power is energy and is converted, as the example of the vehicle traveling along the highway powered by fuel presented above, into movement. The metaphor falls short however, by representing Power as fuel that is inanimate and modulated by an outside source. That is not the case at all! Power is animate and active. The adversary is actively opposing us.

Standing at the perimeter of red-hot coals, I looked around at the people gathered with me preparing to fire walk. We held hands as a woman invoked the spirit of the four directions to be witness to our act, the act of walking across coals so hot they would incinerate any flesh that came into direct contact with them. Curiosity drew me to the edge of the circle. I had no intention of walking across coals with a temperature of 2500+ degrees. I was familiar with fire as a source of energy since I served at the sweat lodge as a fire tender, but being in the lodge didn't bring skin into contact with such extreme temperatures. (Though some might argue that point while seated inside the lodge in the midst of the ceremony!) On this cool spring evening a group of twenty-odd people stood in a circle wondering if they had what it would take to venture onto those glowing coals.

Glad my decision was made earlier, I watched to see who would venture out first. The sweat leader stared with an intensity that would surely seem to have cooled even the hottest of flames as he stood looking down at the circle of red-hot coals. Everyone stood motionless. With a whoop that sounded like a war cry, he strode across the bed of crimson chunks. Quickly, two people followed in his steps.

Suddenly, the heat seemed to have found its way inside of me. A surge of energy raced up and down my body. I felt lightheaded and even woozy. Could I walk on those coals? Without a further thought, I knew that the only thing that would convince me to even try was a sign. But it would have to be a sign that left me in no doubt that I could do the impossible or else I would talk myself out of doing such a rash thing. By this time half a dozen men had walked the coals, shouting and waving wildly as they made it across without mishap. Quick! If the next person to walk those coals were female, I'd follow her!

In the next instant, the sweat leader leaned down to his side and grabbed little six-year-old Natalie. Swinging her onto his shoulders, he strode one more time across the fiery bed. Stunned at the speed at which the sign appeared, I couldn't help but also smile at the irony of "female" being a six year old girl carried on the shoulders of a broad shouldered, six foot tall man. I stared as the sweat leader gently set Natalie down on the other side in the cool grass surrounding the fire ring. Could I do it? I lifted my hands to the dark sky, imploring the vastness above to empower me. Never had I felt adrenaline rush through me at such a speed as to defy even an Indy racecar driver! Without hesitating another moment, I took a step. I followed that step with another, and then another, until I had traversed that twenty-five foot circumference of hot coals on my bare feet! Power is energy! Power had enabled movement; those coals were hot enough to burn flesh off the bone, yet I had walked barefoot on them without harm.

Power Is

An enemy is an opponent, an adversary that has as a goal to prey upon the warrior/sorcerer. Why? That is a most natural question to ask. But asking "why" can easily lead to the assumption of inherent blame and that is not the intent here. Shifting the question to "What" may net less bias in the answer, therefore let's word the question, "What is the reason that Power is a warrior/sorcerer's enemy?"

Introducing the word "prey" is helpful in understanding the answer to the question. The universe is a predatory being. Many people advancing the cause of peace will disagree with that statement and may be turned off by reading it. Peace to them, but it is not in the realm of the warrior/sorcerer to encounter a path with no hunter and no hunted. We are a part of the universe and because of the nature of the universe and our relationship to it we are predatory beings! We prey upon and are preyed upon; the premise is without question for the warrior/sorcerer.

Since the sorcery realm operates with the knowledge that mankind is predatory, we belong to a hierarchy. The unfortunate illusion for most of mankind is that man is at the top of that hierarchy, or food chain. If we change the term "food chain" to "energy chain" immediately man is placed quite a bit lower on the pyramid. Suddenly, man not only has rivals, but also is at greater risk to be out done by those above him who have greater energetic capability. Power is above man on the energy chain. Power is a rival that must be bested in order to advance further in a universe operated on energy. The warrior/sorcerer wants freedom and the only way to attain freedom is to evolve our energetic capabilities.

The tendency for Toltec writers is to secularize Toltec terms and to soften them according to the mood of the times. For anyone trying to get a grasp on unfamiliar terms this is partially understandable. What does "impeccability", "sobriety", or "controlled folly" mean? These are common Toltec terms that are not easily defined. "Power" would seem to be much easier to find a definition for; after all, it is a term we are familiar with in our daily lives. What is the problem in using terminology that is easier to understand? The problem is that by softening terms a risk is created. Try replacing the word "enemy" with gateway, stage, hurdle, or step. Any one of those words doesn't nearly convey the imperative nature of the word "enemy." They lead the warrior/sorcerer away from the elements of danger and risk. They soften the need for action that is requisite for the warrior/sorcerer to make headway on the path. Facing life as a battleground is the only way to evolve as a warrior/sorcerer.

At this critical point, I want to make a distinction. Facing life as a battleground does not have to imply that we are at constant odds with those around us. At times we are at odds with others because people in relationships don't always see eye to eye, but hopefully we are not at odds in an ongoing, chronic manner. No. The battleground I refer to is within our perceptive abilities. We are at odds with who we perceive ourselves to be. We fight our thoughts, our emotions, our beliefs, and our socialization that has told us who and what we are rather than what we can be. The crux of the battleground for the warrior/sorcerer is in what she has been told in comparison to what actually is. Initially, this gap can be tremendously wide but the warrior/sorcerer learns to narrow that gap by bringing who and what she is into alignment with what is experienced in the sorcery realm.

The battleground can take us unaware at first, as it did on my camping trip that fortuitous weekend with Don and Lynn when I glanced over at them seated inside of their tent and they were nowhere to be seen. My mind went into high gear. It was in a battle for its very existence.

"I guess I took longer to pack my things than I thought." Rationalization.

"Maybe I didn't really see them five minutes ago." It was easier to think I was a bit off my rocker than to acknowledge that there was no such thing as time!

"Maybe they took their tent down really quickly." This was a stretch; how much time would it take to disassemble a tent and clear the camping site? It would certainly take longer than the five minutes my head had been poked inside my tent.

My mind was scrambling to explain what had happened—and it could not explain the event. This battleground, which occurs in our minds, implies a need for the warrior/sorcerer's vigilance, awareness, decision-making, and energy use. These actions are the mark of the warrior/sorcerer.

Finally, we conclude with the use of "warrior/sorcerer". A warrior is one who is cognizant of the battle she is involved in. There is congruence with her task and her being; there is no splitting of interests. A warrior has a task to perform and the task is to gain freedom. Freedom is defined as arriving at our fullest perceptual potential, without bias and permutations that limit that potential. That freedom is gained by being a sorcerer, a manipulator of energy, and a shifter of perception. From the spot we are now in to where we can only imagine being is the journey to freedom. It is traveled with utmost vigilance and awareness that the task at hand is difficult at best and impossible at worst but the warrior/sorcerer takes the task to heart. Of the four enemies, Power is the most elusive and seductive, a trickster par excellence. Only as we encounter and interact with Power do we move further toward our goal of freedom.

Standing on the tip of the island overlooking the ocean I gazed down. To my right and below me a hundred feet stood a lighthouse. It stood beckoning to those at sea who might need the strength of its strobe on a dark night. To my left I looked all the way to the horizon following the curve of the island as it meandered along the coast. The mountain range dividing the island from east to west, emerald green drapes in the morning sun was surprisingly free of cloud formations. Glancing down to my more immediate left I could make out the buildings and aquariums of "Sea Life Park." The Pacific Ocean was across the street. Literally. The vastness of the water with its rainbow of blue, aqua, and sea green hues stretched out for miles around me. I was at such a height as to be able to see the coral reefs skirting the lava coast, to watch the current sweeping onto the beach in a rhythm known only to its own, and to wonder at the sea life teeming below the rippled surface. Power spoke.

"If you were a sea creature where would you want to be?"

The juxtaposition of the two abodes was potent. Would I want to live out my life in a safe and secure tank of water, including scheduled daily feedings that would certainly increase my life longevity and protect me from natural foes? Or, would I want to battle out my existence in that unpredictable and awesome vastness before me? To the warrior/sorcerer there is only one option.

Chapter 1 Workout:

Act from the premise that you can answer each and every question presented at the end of each chapter in this book. Doing so will set into motion an engagement with Power. Read each question and answer as quickly as you can, without pondering. This quick response will be less filtered through the mind than if you take time to answer and allow your mind to unduly influence your response.

1. There is something in your life that prevents you from gaining greater freedom. What is it? How will you go about letting go? Does "letting go" for you, mean ending a friendship or relationship, stopping an activity, or changing thought patterns?

2. Write out your definition of Power. Try not to look back in the chapter in order to get the answer but write from your own understanding of the term at this time.

3. Identify a time when Power has acted upon you.

4. Looking back in hindsight on your life's experiences, is there an experience that you can "decode" as one of Power acting on you?

5. "What kind of Power do you use?" Looking at our life experiences in a new light will allow us to see what we've previously missed.

6. The battleground we encounter as warrior/sorcerers is within our perceptive capabilities that have been too easily relegated to our minds. These perceptive capabilities can often be determined by what we pay attention to. Identify a battle you encounter within this realm.

7. Choose a time and place wherein you can invite Power to engage with you. Even though you may find as you read along that you have engaged with Power already, (which is most likely the case) this experience will set your intent on a conscious level to either begin your encounter with Power or to develop it further.

2.
The Enemy

Looking down I notice the river rocks that intermingle with the gentle mountain stream. The water gurgles and trips over the stones heading out of view into a pine forest that surrounds me. I lift my eyes to notice a woman standing on the rocky shore. Standing tall and quiet she is veritable stillness itself; she stands without moving but it is her spirit that lends the air of magic to her presence. A teacher. She is watching me.

"It is time to go to the eight sacred circles," she announces. My heart skips and tumbles as though it is the water suddenly bouncing along the bed of stones. I've been waiting for this moment! Years of training and finally I am ready to take this next step along the path.

"Would you draw me a map?" I say, reaching for a small branch and handing it to her. "Draw it for me right here in the dirt," I suggest, "that way I can find them easier." Her look changes instantly. With piercing intensity she gazes at me. Abruptly, I am confused. Paralyzed by her stare, I dare not utter another word.

"Stay here instead, there is still more for you to learn." With nary a rustle in the breeze she is gone. Alone I stand in the mountain glen not at all sure of what had just taken place.

An act of force involving subterfuge and attack took the country by surprise September 11, 2001. To this day, six years later, the United States continues to be offended that a third world country militia attacked our country and succeeded with their violent intent. By rerouting two planes into the World Trade Center the enemy succeeded at a plan never before attempted. The planes exploded inside the Twin Towers in New York City causing an implosion that decimated those one hundred story buildings within an hour. Stunned Americans stood by helpless, their eyes affixed to their televisions as the towers appeared to tumble and fall like a house of cards alighted by flames. Regardless of the opinion about which country was "right or wrong" (as though that could be accurately determined) amongst the opponents, everyone agrees that an act of power was imposed against a country of power. A very powerful plan was conceived against a very powerful country, and reverberations from that attack continue to this day. The event, tragic as it was, provides the warrior/sorcerer with a powerful example!

Something is terribly amiss. Whether what is amiss is the moral ideal of the attackers or the lack of preparedness by the attacked is up for speculation, but what can be questioned is how knowledgeable the opposing sides were of each other. How thoroughly did the power sources know each other? How much information did they have on each other that indicated an attack of such magnitude was in the making or that they even had the wherewithal to pull the attack off? Had we studied our enemy sufficiently to anticipate their every move? Had the enemy studied us sufficiently to anticipate our every move? The grand clash of Power highlights for the warrior/sorcerer the imperative of knowing the enemy. There is no room for error when dealing with Power of such magnitude. Both sides apparently didn't take that risk fully into account.

All this talk of enemies can put the reader off, to say the least. After all, we are civilized people who can come to the proverbial round table and make informed decisions. Sadly, in light of 9/11 and its aftermath, that statement is as far from the truth as the earth is from the moon. (Neither are we limited to that one event. There are a dozen other events our country has involved itself with in the past one hundred years that point to our predatory nature.) We delude ourselves into believing we are civilized; our actions certainly show we are not. Besides, we are talking about warrior/sorcerers in the Toltec context and not that of the common man. This context is all the more reason that we acknowledge our nature and act accordingly.

The warrior/sorcerer's nature is predatory. It is in the nature of a predatory creature to have a deadline in which to act. If a predatory creature doesn't hunt prey for sustenance within a certain time frame, they will die. It is also a certainty that it's only a matter of time before prey larger than the creature itself will be victorious in the hunt. It is the same for the warrior/sorcerer. All creatures, including human beings, face a natural enemy. We know who that prey is, although we don't want to think about it often. Death. The deadline for the warrior/sorcerer in which to gain her own freedom is her Death. Every living creature faces Death in one way or another, but for the warrior/sorcerer Death changes from a gruesome, fearful event to a living, daily presence. When our daily actions are based on the realization that Death can be one moment away rather than a lifetime away, our actions take on a different meaning. At the very heart of Toltec awareness is this: Death is imminent! Death is a proximal event, not a future one. Recognizing the immediacy of a viable exchange with Death will transform our lives! How many people have we read about that have a near death experience (NDE) and their lives are forever changed? Death rearranges priorities.

With my foot on the break, I slowed the car down on the canyon road. The fog enveloped my surroundings so completely that fifteen feet ahead of me looked like a block of solid white wall. I had traveled the road plenty of times during daylight but never at 4:45 a.m. in the morning. The car's headlights only served to make the wall of fog in front of me impenetrable. Glancing quickly out the window, I wondered if the canyon road had any electrical light poles but as I drove past a pole without light, I realized that the electricity must be on a timer, and the lighting was already off for the day. I was heading toward the canyon trails that I had recently been hiking as often as I could. It seemed to me that during a hike, the trail would speak, and as a consequence, I had begun to pose my dilemmas to the trail on a regular basis. (The earth we live on has much to share with us!) This morning I wanted to pose a question about Power, and it was imperative to pose the question while it was still dark. There was something about darkness that enabled me to perceive differently. The combination of darkness and the trail would do the trick, I was sure.

This plan sounded good while lying in bed the night before, but now I was afraid. Suddenly, I remembered every person who had ever warned me about hiking the canyon alone. "Didn't you hear about the cougar that was caught last week in Riverside? It's the dry season and they come down from the hills to find water." "You hike without a partner? Kind of dangerous isn't it?" "You know, I saw two bobcats last week in the next canyon over." Smitten with the memory of all of the comments, I began to feel foolish. How would I protect myself from cougars, bobcats, wild dogs, and any other kind of animal whose territory I was trespassing? Besides, what was I really trying to accomplish anyway? I slowed the car even further. That damn fog was getting thicker. Could I even find the trail in this fog?

Without warning, a dull thud hit the right front fender. I'd hit something! Immediately, the right front tire rolled over the object and just as quickly as the back tire followed, the car rolled over the object a second time. My foot hit the brake pedal. With a knowing that I was beginning to recognize with uncanny certainty, I knew what had happened. I had hit a jackrabbit. I must turn around and go home! I didn't have the Power it takes to hunt Power! How could I kill an animal through such foolishness? Yet despite knowing that I had caused the death of the jackrabbit, I knew I would continue up the canyon road. I had an appointment with Power that morning. Even though Death was present—viable—at that very moment, I pushed my foot down on the accelerator.

Death will realign our relationship with Power. It will put Power into the context of the enemy that it is. If we are truly aware that at a moment in time we have an appointment with Death, we will quickly recognize that Power as an enemy will divert our attention from that inescapable appointment with Death. Because we cannot afford to sacrifice ourselves to Death, we must reiterate over and over that Power is an enemy. Power will keep us from facing Death on a daily basis and cause us to act as though we have a lifetime in which to act, to get things together, and to do what we truly want to do. Consequently, when we have a lifetime in which to act, we tend to live in the future rather than living in the moment at hand. We put off until tomorrow what may only be possible to do today.

Our mind wants to rid ourselves of the rough edge implied in the statement, "Power is an Enemy." It wants to tumble and toss it about to smooth the edges as a tumbler does a stone. If Power is soft and smooth then it will demand less of us should there be any contact. Our mind cannot fathom the necessity of facing Power as an enemy because of the consequences if we do. If Power is truly a formidable enemy our task is to be knowledgeable about its nature, and vigilant about its every move directed our way. That task cannot be relegated to a weekend endeavor, a cursory attempt, or mild mannered report. The task calls for strategic, mindful, and fastidious attention. This attention is all that the warrior/sorcerer has to give.

We know we must face an enemy but the enemy is a stranger to us. How can we study an enemy we know nothing about? Remember, Power will teach us about Power. It comes to challenge us, and in that challenge Power defines and enlarges our capacity for knowing itself. "Understanding" is not the word to use; we don't want to understand Power. We want to know what Power is and how it challenges us; after all, the Toltec path is all about action.

An immutable Toltec law that provides us with our bearings to get started is stated thus: in order to engage with Power we *must have* Power. The statement sounds simple and obvious; no need for all this talk about how dangerous an enemy is this Power! If that were indeed the case, that the law is a simple one, an easily grasped concept, we wouldn't have any quandary or concern about interacting when Power does show up. Simply meet Power with Power! It turns out that this is exactly what we do, but alas, warrior/sorcerers don't always know they have Power to begin with! They are not familiar with Power in all its manifestations. Power starts out a mystery by grafting and contorting and shape shifting to keep the warrior/sorcerer on her toes. The hunted seldom lies down in the arms of the hunter.

Watch for the emphasis on the word "must have" in the law. It is not stating that the warrior/sorcerer must by all means grapple to get Power to start her battle with Power. Rather, refer back to the first Toltec law, found in the first paragraph of the introduction, stating that the warrior/sorcerer goes into the very bosom of Power itself because it is the purpose of the journey to do so. The warrior/sorcerer can go there because she has the Power to go there; it is a given, it is not a "must get." When I stepped onto those fiery coals during the fire walk, I did so because Power indicated I had the capability to walk on them without being harmed. I was exercising an inherent capability whether or not I was cognizant of doing so in that very moment when the body's natural adrenaline surged through me and catapulted me into that circle of fire.

What the warrior/sorcerer must begin to do regardless of how much awareness she has of her own Power is to act on what she knows in the moment. She recognizes that she has the Power to engage with Power—no matter how much or how little she possesses—and the recognition gets her started. Power will find a way to enlarge her energetic capacity; it is in its nature to do so. "Must have" is not in the future; it is a current state of being. The warrior/sorcerer already has Power with which to meet this most formidable enemy!

When a warrior/sorcerer knows and anticipates an encounter with Power she also knows what to do to be prepared. If you don't know that's the purpose for reading this book. There is a "quiver of arrows" that can be slung on your back, and a bow in your hand fitted with an arrow to get you started. This chapter will introduce you to two important tasks for the warrior/sorcerer to begin doing now and the remainder of the book will introduce you to a handful of others.

In addition, we will look at one other method of preparation that can easily be overlooked due to its apparently passive nature. It turns out that the last tool for the warrior/sorcerer is all about strategizing and hence it is vital for success. Even though it may appear passive, it concerns planning, critical thinking, and even repetition, because one of the ways

Encounter with Power

in which we learn to go into battle is to be aware of what has gone on before us. First, let's look at two primary tools for the warrior/sorcerer.

Primary tools for battle are Tracking and Dreaming. They are presented here in somewhat different format than may be familiar for a reader of Toltec literature. The word choices themselves remain the same; it is difficult if not impossible to design new terms that encompass all that these two terms already imply. At this juncture they will be introduced as though the reader is a first year undergrad, but with the understanding that the terms can easily be explored as post-doctoral specialties. Each term in itself can be explored with the precision and singularity of a microphysicist studying a chain of DNA. As is true for all Toltec endeavors, once the warrior/sorcerer gets a handle on them, those endeavors take on a life of their own and begin to be the instructor and guide, acting as energetic forces that abound in the universe. A written account serves to introduce the concept. Because words act as a diving board, it is up to the reader to launch off the platform and enter into the depth of the actual experience for him or herself. If they do not, they are simply observers seated on a narrow plank and the end result will be to deprive themselves of entering the depth of experience available within their eyesight.

Tracking (or "Stalking" as it is termed equally often) is the art of observing yourself and your world, including people, places and things, and then making decisions based on what is observed. Action is called for at every turn of the road even if it is the decision to be still and quiet. The Toltec world is all about decision making to a certain point because we are working in the world of everyday life or common reality. Down the road, decision making comes without thought because the warrior/sorcerer has developed it to the point that every move is in perfect harmony with who the warrior/sorcerer is, but for now decision making is oftentimes a definite thought moving into action. Even though the warrior/sorcerer's goal may be to end up in another world altogether, she is at present an intricate player in the known world. Being familiar with this common world is a result of making decisions early on to by-pass the warrior/sorcerer's realm. We have trained ourselves not to see what we don't want to see, and it becomes a matter of retraining ourselves to see what is right before our very noses. It is a matter of working backwards to return to our former awareness. In order to do so we begin to make decisions that will dismantle what we know. We dismantle the known to get back to the unknown, knowing that both the known and the unknown are equal players. This concept is much like the statement made earlier that "the world" and "the sorcerer's realm" are one and the same; it may take some time to unravel in order to fully assimilate. The known and the unknown are equal qualities faced by the warrior/sorcerer. They need balanced attention placed on them because it is tempting to want to go after high adventure or "bells and whistles". These kinds of events trigger adrenalin rush much like the earlier example of fire walking. Power comes in the known and the unknown realms; it is no respecter of worlds, so the warrior/sorcerer must be fluid and fluent in both.

There are other acts that operate in the Tracking arena. These include acts based on awareness: our use of time, resources, talents; patterns in behavior toward self and others; interactions in relationships; what, when, and to whom we pay attention; alternatives taken and those not taken, and stream-of-consciousness. We're paying attention to all internal and external "doings" or those things we do, think, say, and feel. Whew! It's an exhausting list of things to pay attention to, but we cannot make definitive decisions unless we become fully aware of exactly what it is we're working with from the outset.

Belonging to a sweat lodge group was a chapter in my life that taught me many things about the fire, the stones, "fire tenders" or those who carry the stones into the lodge, people who gather at such events, and relationships. Toward the end of my time with the group a gentleman approached me to inquire why I was no longer going to participate. I told him why I was leaving. He encouraged me to stay a bit longer.

"You are a strong presence here but you need to speak up more. I've listened to what you have to say but you don't say it loud enough. You become a chameleon when others speak up righteously for their point of view. That's when I would love to hear your voice instead of you backing down." I was astounded.

Tracking what he had to say by reflecting on my time with the group, aware that his comments had been unsolicited, and observing that everything occurring within my field of influence had potential to impact my energy state, I paid attention. Piecing together several other events at the sweat lodge that related to my voice and what he was saying, I began to do exactly as he advised. It was a decision that went against the grain of who I perceive myself to be and yet there were too many signs flagging my attention to be ignored. It was time to exercise personal power through my voice, which involved changing my usually quiet demeanor, thereby acting in a manner that changed my known. Tracking was taking me into the unknown while changing my known at the same time. This is the first mention of personal power. It is a term with which we will involve ourselves more a little further down the road, but for now, know that a goal for the warrior/sorcerer is to take Power and to claim it for her use.

Dreaming is the second primary tool for a warrior/sorcerer. If Tracking is done in the day, Dreaming is at the other end of the time spectrum and is performed during the night. Although this is not necessarily always true, because Tracking and Dreaming occur any time and anywhere whether awake or asleep, for now an introductory concept is the idea that Dreaming occurs at night during the dreamtime. A distinction is also made between dreaming and Dreaming; one is the images that can occupy during our theta sleep and that we often interpret and work with, and the other is Dreaming in which another part of us comes to life and begins to act by traveling, interacting with energies initially unfamiliar to us, and gathering Power in acts previously unfamiliar to us. It is the stuff of other worlds.

Before the warrior/sorcerer does any Dreaming, the definition of the term benefits them little. It is an act so outside of our everyday life that to conceive of it takes Power in itself! The warrior/sorcerer begins to go over and over these concepts like a hungry dog to a bone. No matter that you don't understand them or are unable to describe them! Begin to pay attention to your dreaming. In the psychoanalytic world, dreaming is the royal road to the unconscious. In the Toltec world Dreaming is the royal road to Power. The emphasis so far has been on Power as an enemy and that will continue; at the same time we will begin to shift our perspective and begin to emphasize the benefits Power has to offer.

Lucid dreaming is the open door to Dreaming proper. My first lucid dream was wildly exciting, even though I was clueless that what I was doing was developing my capacity to engage with Power. I simply thought I was taking my Dreaming to the next level, that of volitional choice. The details of the dream are individual to the dreamer, they merely serve as clothing to the body of Dreaming, but they are provided in order to highlight the act that being lucid serves, in other words, engagement with Power.

Early one morning I awoke as I heard my daughter leave for swim practice. Pleased that I had an hour or so to return to dreaming, I rolled over in bed and lay very still. I wondered whether or not I could return to sleep, or whether my mind would become too active in thinking about my schedule for the rest of the day. In front of me, in my direct line of vision, I noticed several cars parked along an incline. One of them was rolling down the hill backward, picking up speed as it moved. Engrossed in the movement of the speeding car, I stared wide-eyed, as the car approached the bottom of the hill. Without a conscious shift in my awareness, I asked, "I wonder if I'm going to start dreaming?"

"Dummy, you were dreaming. Remember the car?" I continued to lay still. If I didn't move my body an inch, maybe I could return to the dream state.

Suddenly, I was in the home of an acquaintance, a woman from the Institute where I attended school. Seated at a small table, we were enjoying a cup of tea. Around us in the large kitchen, a crew was finishing preparations for a party.

"I'm dreaming," I said to myself.

A dozen women were wandering the house, waiting for the buffet to be prepared, after which there was to be a lecture from the workshop speaker. Rising from the tea table, I walked down the hallway, heading toward the conference room.

"I'm dreaming," I said again.

"To prove that I am dreaming, I will blink my eyes, and the shoes on my feet will change." Blink. Different shoes were on my feet. Blink. Another pair of shoes was now on my feet. Walking down the hallway, I blinked, changed shoes, blinked, changed shoes, blinked, and changed shoes again.

"I'd like a different suit on, too." Blink. I had on a brand new dress suit.

"This is a dream. I can construct it in any way that I want—and, I'd like to be the speaker for the workshop!" Cocky and confident, I continued down the hallway, heading toward the conference room. Upon awakening, I returned again and again to the feeling of being in the dreaming state. Such a feeling of liveliness and vitality! A feeling of total immersion in the moment at hand, as though nothing else in the world mattered. All of my attention was placed on the significance of the moment at hand; it appeared as though I could create whatever reality I desired in that precious moment. What Power!

Dreaming is a tool warrior/sorcerers wield in order to develop their "energy body," or Other, as it is also called. Reading the above Dreaming story, it is easy to say, "What does changing your shoes in a dream have to do with developing the Other?" Fair question. Remember, the warrior/sorcerer enters another cognition when she is Dreaming; she is outside of what she knows of the daily world. Energetic awareness travels back and forth between Dreaming and the daily world and the accrual of that energy is what develops the Other. Therefore, any act of Dreaming, regardless of content, builds on our investment. Because we are welded to the daily world of everyday life, we have scant opportunity to develop our energetic capacities to the extent that can be developed through Dreaming. If left to our physical bodies to perform, we wouldn't have the energy necessary to accomplish the most desirable of Toltec acts, developing the Other. But Dreaming gives us the avenue that is absolutely critical in order to accomplish this act. It is a complex art, but the warrior/sorcerer, regardless of where she is on the path, grooms her self into a position to do Dreaming.

These two arts, as they can be termed, are fundamental to encountering Power. They hone our awareness to what Power is and what Power does as they increase our perception or our ability to perceive energy and, above all, the warrior/sorcerer is focused on her energy expenditure. Only with enough energy can we face the unknown and challenge our Death. With enough practice the warrior/sorcerer uses Tracking and Dreaming to turn her world upside down.

Historically, a warrior/sorcerer claimed herself as either a Tracker or a Dreamer, but in these times it is imperative to develop both skills without a preference. An analogy would be gender. If we are male or female makes little difference where energy is concerned. Eons ago (if we believe in a yesteryear) mankind was androgynous, having both male and female reproductive organs. Eons ago warrior/sorcerers were equal Tracker and Dreamers, there was no preference for the dual arts, but times and modalities have changed. For centuries, the sexes are, and have been, clearly delineated, although even that distinction is slowly losing its relevance (in an eventual return to the androgynous state). The distinction between a Tracker and a Dreamer is following in the same manner.

A warrior/sorcerer in today's times must develop both skills without the distinction of claiming one or the other as her strength. Few have the luxury of devoting time and energy to one art alone. We are dealing with two worlds: the daily world of "reality", and the world of the sorcerer's realm. As a quick preview, Tracking deals with daily reality and Dreaming deals with altered reality; even then, we are aiming to practice both skills in both worlds fluidly.

Finally, we have arrived at the last of the warrior/sorcerers arrows that fill her quiver. Earlier the question was asked, "How can we study an enemy we know nothing about?" The answer comes from an unlikely source: storytelling. Specifically, the warrior/sorcerer listens or reads about the way other warrior/sorcerers have handled and battled with Power. The strategy in doing so is to learn from the experience gained by those before us who have Tracked and Dreamed their way to freedom. It sounds inactive, even passive for the reader or listener, yet for centuries storytelling has captured the hearts and minds of those listening.

There are two reasons a warrior/sorcerer is interested in hearing other warrior/sorcerer stories. First, there is a large, patterned, repetitious part of us that goes along for the ride when we travel. That part of us is our mind. Our mind is diametrically opposed to the path we have set for ourselves as warrior/sorcerers. In a sense, from the beginning our mind has been taxed with a job that it was never intended to perform and yet, despite a change in our mindset, the mind wants to continue its appointed task. As the warrior/sorcerer continues on the Toltec path, the mind will take a back seat to those functions that are reawakened within us. The mind's functioning will shift and change. Even then our mind will concede to change only if it doesn't feel threatened. If we make an enemy of our mind we will be fighting two battles, one with our mind and one with Power: a sure route to defeat.

But if we enlist our mind and provide it with thought as fodder, in a sense educating it, we can attend to the battle at hand with Power. Too often our mind is made into a thousand headed monster and the battle is on to dethrone it after the warrior/sorcerer finally discovers its true occupation. But these efforts are unnecessary. The mind doesn't need eradicating; it needs to be doing the job it was intended to do rather than doing what it has been coaxed to do by those without a warrior/sorcerer's purpose. Given a false dictum, "Run the show," the mind has taken over executive functions it is not qualified to perform. When a warrior/sorcerer realigns job duties to the body, mind, and spirit on a more even basis, the mind continues to operate but in a more selective manner. Storytelling is an endeavor that will occupy the mind.

The following story is about the mind, while at the same time, it is a story about Death. Some experiences don't transliterate well into language. This story fits that category. But it is important to read anyway! This story will stand you in good stead until you have your own story to tell about your own mind, and how Death bypasses it. Death was beginning to advise me. Death was setting my priorities straight and I was finding out that those priorities had little to do with my mind.

I lie in bed early one Sunday morning thinking about my experience at the sweat lodge the evening before. Three words had swirled around my head all evening, and they continued in bed with me in the early morn. I was thinking about "meaning", "understanding", and "knowing". Those three words had served me well in my psychoanalytic days. It was the job, even duty, of the analyst to assist the client in gaining meaning and understanding to their life experience, to altar the way that they perceived the events in their lives that held sway over them. And— "knowing?" Well, knowing something gave me a sense of certainty and assuredness that the meaning and understanding I gave to an experience was on target and was of significance to either myself, or to my client. I cherished those three words—and yet—sweating last night had given me a different slant to them. Those three words were heavy and encumbering! They occupied so much of my time even thinking about them! Much of what I did was wrapped up in those three words.

An image of the shoes Liza wore the day before floated across my mental screen. Cute! I had even asked her where she'd gotten them in order to get a pair for myself. Slowly, I drifted into a dream. In the dream, I found three pairs of sandals in the back of my closet that I used to wear. I picked up the pair of brown, woven ones, and put them on.

"Ah! Comfortable!" I murmured. I remembered wearing them all day long. I was glad to have a pair of sandals that were so suitable to my needs and taste. "Maybe I should wear these sandals, rather than go to the expense of getting another pair? After all, these fit me perfectly. Maybe I'll just keep these." I shifted in the bed, and came halfway out of the dream state.

Without thinking, I lay motionless. My mind was still, as I lay listening to the sounds of the coming day. No words, no thoughts, no images—nothing came to mind. Nothing at all. Blackness surrounded me. Not merely the blackness of having my eyes closed, but a deeper, blacker black prevailed. The blackness had depth to it, as though I had entered a pitch-dark room, and I could feel the size of the dark. It was immense. I lay as though paralyzed in the stillness. Suddenly, with a clarity that leaves no doubt whatsoever, an odd thought came to me, as though it was traveling at the velocity of the speed of light.

"Ohhhhh!" The exclamation was drawn out, exaggerated and breathless.

"Death is on its way!" The comfort at knowing that Death was near was no less comforting than a babe in its mother's arms; it was profound immunity from any kind of harm. All was well. Death was alive! Not only was Death conscious, it consumed all that came into contact with it; there was no escape. Death was a victor that left no survivors. Foreboding set in. Death was too big, too overpowering, for me to fend off. I didn't stand a chance! I groaned, writhing on the bed in terror. Frightened, my mind went into action.

"Wait a minute! What just happened? I experienced something, but what was it?" Instant amnesia nearly eclipsed the experience. I lay in bed, my mind groping for meaning and understanding, those old "shoes" that were so comfortable to wear. "Was it something about Death?" I felt the weight of my thoughts stacking on top of each other, weighing in to assist, clouding, and obscuring the moment before in order to help put definition to it. My mind was clumsy. The words had no dexterity, a giant oaf attempting a pirouette. The more my mind tried to put any pictures, metaphor, and words to the experience, the farther it escaped me. For the rest of the day, I felt out of sorts, out of time, without definition. I was no longer sure of what I knew, or how to explain myself. Death was reordering my thinking.

There is a second reason that the warrior/sorcerer is interested in the stories of other warrior/sorcerers. Hearing stories of those warrior/sorcerers who have battled before will provide us a map with which to travel. Their strategies can either become ours, or be avoided by us at any costs. A paradox of the Toltec path is this: countless warrior/sorcerers have given their lives in the pursuit of freedom. They go before us with either their victories or failures as our example. At the same time, the only way to travel this path is by personal experience and by taking action on what we know or don't know. There is no other way! The wise warrior/sorcerer will avail her self of both. Reading about other warrior/

sorcerers and their battle with Power will show us what Power is, how to arm ourselves against it, when to approach or recede, where the battle will take place, and who we might come into contact with during the fray.

There are a dozen prominent Toltec authors on the market. There is also a foolproof method to determine which author or authors will act as a guide to the path. It is this: the books will come to you! Believe it or not—the path is strewn with storytellers! Regardless of how a story of Power comes to you, whether recommended, online, or in the bookstore, written records of warrior/sorcerers are out there. Some of them are worth reading, and reading repeatedly. Others may write in a style or genre that doesn't suit your tastes. That fact shouldn't hinder you from finding one that does. Centuries ago warrior/sorcerers passed down their escapades through oral tradition. Nowadays, warrior/sorcerers commit their acts to the written word. Either way, stories are being handed down from warrior/sorcerers on the path battling and handling Power that will act as guide and mentor. Be aware. Open your eyes. It will happen. There is no better way, apart from entering your own battle, to prepare for an encounter with Power than to read and hear from others having similar experiences. Resist making your mind an enemy. Enlist it instead to do a job it is up to the task to perform, and to perform well.

The island cliff side was beautiful beyond anything I'd seen. We stood at the top and gazed out upon the Pacific Ocean stretching miles before us rippling and curling upon itself in shades of azure, cobalt, and royal blue. The sky was clean and clear with a blueness that extended into eternity. The day was sparkling with a vividness unseen in Southern California, my home state for forty some years. The previous day I had flown to Hawaii and left the biting cold, California winter. I was in Hawaii to visit my daughters for the Christmas holidays.

"And this is the middle of December," I murmured as I reminded myself that I was wearing shorts and a tank top.

Turning around I looked back at the path through the Ironwood trees that we had just crossed. Between the path and the cliff side was a medicine wheel, a "heiau," or place of energy to the Hawaiian people. The perimeter was lava stone placed side by side which then dissected the circle at 45-degree angles to

Encounter with Power

meet in the middle, making the huge circle a roulette wheel—of chance or fate or opportunity—Power would decide. Small wildflowers scattered the grass as though strewn from a goddess' flick of the wrist.

Respectfully, we walked to the center of the great wheel. A four-foot high lava stone was graced with leis, shells, woven grass, bits of glass, and coins. A place of Power! I trembled.

"Come on, Mom. The tide pool can only be reached by going over the side of the cliff. The only way to get there is by letting ourselves down this rope. It's awesome!" My two young adult daughters lived in Hawaii while taking a semester off from college. The magic of the islands had called to them and they wanted to share the magic with me while I was here for the week. We began our descent.

Plummeting straight down before us was the lava precipice leading to the ocean pool. Sculpted from lava and replenished with each crashing wave, the pool looked like a giant sapphire set amidst a lacy network of steel gray filigree. I kneeled down and grasped the rope hanging over the edge. Weathered, it had knots every eighteen inches or so and dropped to a length of nearly twenty feet.

As I lowered myself, holding onto those knots for dear life, my breathing stopped. Shuddering, I realized that without the rope strategically placed on the cliff side, there was no possibility of lowering a human body down. How strong was this twine with the gnarled knots placed along its length? The girls encouraged me, but I could feel my fear rising. With sweaty palms and furrowed brow I lowered myself one knot at a time, carefully placing my shoes on the rough surface of the lava. I could easily have sat in the center of the heiau while the girls went swimming in the pool. At the same time, I admitted to myself that there was an unseen force that dragged me down that cliff side. Against any sane, rational judgment I lowered myself down, down, finally reaching the great pool. Lowering my body into the crystal blue water, I quickly looked for some handhold in case I needed a steadying influence.

"Mom, look out, a wave's coming!" I heard the voice a second too late. With uncommon force a wave hit the pool and exploded. Instantly, I was underwater and slammed against the steel gray filigree that had looked so beautiful from twenty feet higher. One knee hit the lava and my hands grabbed wildly for support to steady myself. As the wave rebounded my body slammed *into the lava edge again. The girls saw the wave coming; they dove into the depths of the pool just before it hit. I was battered and bruised with flesh ragged and torn on my feet, hands, and knees. Blood gushed through the wounds as though running through a sieve.*

I burst into tears. The Power of that place had chewed me up and spit me out! I was afraid and uncertain. So this was Power unprepared for, Power unheeded! How naïve: that I thought Power would only be found in the vortex of the medicine wheel above!

Chapter 2 Workout:

1. "In order to engage with Power we must have Power." What Power do you have at this moment? Acknowledge the Power that you have; this very Power will bring more Power to you. Watch for it!

2. How deeply have you engaged with Dreaming at this time in your life? In what way is Power active in your Dreaming? If it is not, invite Power into your Dreaming.

3. How deeply have you engaged with Tracking at this time in your life? In what way is Power active in your Tracking? If it is not, invite Power into your Tracking.

4. "Countless warrior/sorcerers have given their lives in the pursuit of freedom." Identify a warrior/sorcerer you know that has given their life in the pursuit of freedom. Learn as much as you can about that person. They can provide you with a treasure store of examples and stories from which knowledge can be gleaned.

5. How have you allowed Death to reorder your thinking? It is important to be aware of how you are viewing Death—you want to be actively engaged with Death and not merely passively observant of it. Speak to Death; find out where you stand regarding Death in your life at this time.

6. Where are you looking for Power? Power can be found anywhere! Begin to notice Power in places you have not seen it before.

3.
Accessible To Power

Arriving at my third chakra I was aware that it was the energy wheel of my emotions and the seat of my intellectual thought. Bright yellow in color, the chamber I entered was gargantuan. Towering above me, while simultaneously appearing mobile along the ground, were huge blocks arranged to form a maze. They appeared to have the inherent ability to shift and to move at will. The blocks were clearly my emotions and moods. A narrow path could barely be discerned between two of the blocks and looked as though it was leading into the maze itself.

A voice commented, "The passageway needs to be wider so that when the blocks shift there won't be any danger of them crushing you." I took a step into the narrow pathway. The sheer size of the blocks created the sensation of walking along a narrow street in New York City with towering buildings on either side hiding any available light from the sun.

"If your emotions and moods weren't so dominant the trail would be more easily traversed and sun and wind could travel with you along the path." I walked along slowly pondering what the voice had said.

"The blocks used to be totally jammed, like logs downstream to the mill or a word rebus that can't be maneuvered because it's stuck in a track," the voice explained.

"In your field of endeavor, it is desirable to be able to recognize and identify the emotions. In the Toltec world the emotions are not the Prima Donna of the psyche."

Encounter with Power

Feeling claustrophobic, I could feel the monoliths move ever so slightly. With a gasp, I recognized that what the voice had just told me was all too true: the width and length of the passageway gave no opportunity for escape should the blocks slide into each other. I listened as the voice continued.

"When you get stuck in one of your moods, you are in a dangerous position of becoming immobile or even of being crushed. These blocks include your moods, your emotions and your intellect."

The voice chuckled, "No accident that you are seeing them as giant blocks. It is time to realize they are not who you are; it is time to let them go."

When first walking the Toltec path as a warrior/sorcerer it is difficult to recognize Power, as we have already discovered. We have also discovered that Power will make itself known to us because it's in its nature to do so. Meanwhile, the warrior/sorcerer has a task of monumental significance. It is a task of such magnitude that it will take much of her time and available energy due to its very significance. Metaphorically the task would be to shrink the size of the blocks in the yellow cavern from the above dreaming story.

Picture yourself standing within inches of the massive blocks; they tower a dozen stories above you while being suspended off the ground by inches, thus giving them maneuverability. They shift and slide, groaning with their very weight and volume, moving slowly but inexorably in your direction. The path is narrow, there is no place to hide or run for escape. What do you do? The task pictured is the same task every warrior/sorcerer finds her self in position to confront. Traditionally it is called "lessening self importance." The task is to shrink the space and volume of the blocks and therefore their dominance in our world. Unless we are able to accomplish this task there will be no room in the form of Power to engage with us at all.

We are building upon our knowledge base. Already, we are eager to face Power but are now being told that another task takes precedence. It is easy to view the two tasks, battling Power and lessening self-importance, as strangers to each other but thankfully this is not the case. What this seeming disparity addresses is a Toltec mystery and there are many mysteries on this path. As we engage in lessening our self-importance we are carving out space for Power to enter. Even though we may not be facing Power directly, it is stealthily approaching us and amassing strength from behind our backs. Oddly, Power has the quality of building unnoticed while we are engaged in alternative tasks. This is the mystery. Once a warrior/sorcerer recognizes the signs of Power she is able to observe its effects in her life. Hindsight provides us a clearer view.

Immediately, because we have taken to heart that Power is an enemy, we question how this can be. How can we turn our backs on an enemy of such eminence, much less turn to something as innocuous as "self-importance" while doing so? Even the question reveals how inaccurately we may be viewing our self-importance. It dominates our lives to the point that it squeezes out any other focus or attention; it is the mammoth block that narrows the path to a scant dribble, crowded and coerced to the size of a self-starving adolescent. Unless the blocks are shriveled there will be no movement and, therefore, no battle with Power at all. The concern is not that we will be so engaged elsewhere that Power will go away. Power will meet us when it is time. Its purpose is not to crush us without our awareness, but to approach us as an honorable enemy prepared to engage us head on. We can place our confidence in this: Power builds unnoticed while we prepare ourselves for the encounter by lessening our self-importance!

The idea that human beings have self-importance is not a difficult concept to agree with or to observe. Human beings parade their self-importance in a myriad of ways unique to each and every one of us. The feeling of grandiosity and "specialness" runs the gambit from demure coyness to flaming narcissism. We can all observe the self-importance that others display on a daily basis. What is tough to grasp is the extent to which the importance of the self has infiltrated our society and in turn oneself. The "self" is celebrated, particularly in Western culture, and has been put on a pedestal for all to emulate for a hundred or more years. Early psychologists began to advance the notion of a self and promote it with a desirable spin, hence we have "self concept," "self esteem," and "self image," at one end of the spectrum of psychological health. At the other end of the spectrum we have "self aggrandizement," "self effacement," and "self promoting," terms denoting a wounded or inflated sense of self that are looked upon with a raised and judgmental eye. We even have the term "selfless" promoted as a desired way of being in many esoteric schools.

With all of this varied emphasis on the self how does the warrior/sorcerer address her self-importance? How does the warrior/sorcerer begin to address this abstract concept that is blocking her contact with Power? Let's first take a closer look at "self" and how it might manifest in our lives before we talk about ridding ourselves of it due to its importance. There are two "selves" that every warrior/sorcerer deals with on a daily basis. One self is a tyrant, a bully, and a taskmaster. The second self is the one we want to nurture and to develop. One self we want to tame and to eventually move away from. The second self is true to who we are as energetic beings. We want this second self to grow in order for it not to be easily confused with the first self. The first self we'll put into quotes: "self." The second self we'll leave to stand on its' own without parenthesis, in order to differentiate between the two.

The "self" is a construct of the mind. It is the person we think and believe ourselves to be as we enter the Toltec path. It is our socialized persona, the personality traits we have come to recognize as who we are. In order to survive in a predatory universe, this "self" has taken on a sense of importance that knows no bounds. This "self" is often identified with the ego, that mental construct of the mind that is given full rights to executive functions. This "self" is the autocrat that runs the show.

The second self has little to do with the mind. It has been abandoned in the pursuit of the "self." Once we recognize that we have this second self, abandoned at birth to the whims and fancy of the "self", we can begin to attend to this part of us that we have ignored. Initially, the two are difficult to differentiate. Once they can be more clearly differentiated it is tempting to want to rid our selves of the "self." But we don't want to rid ourselves of the "self" entirely because it serves a purpose for the warrior/sorcerer.

I was vested for several years into a doctoral program when I began to experiment with Shamanic journeying and drumming, the Tarot, sweat lodge, and Chi Gong body—work. I hadn't yet identified myself as a warrior/sorcerer in the Toltec tradition even though I was in the playing field of altered perceptions. While at a weeklong workshop in Montana one fall, a fellow participant did a reading for me with a Tarot deck she had designed and created herself. Being unfamiliar with Tarot decks of any kind, I listened to her words as she described to me what she was seeing in the cards.

"You are being bedeviled by something, what is it?" She pointed to a card in the center of the spread that clearly depicted a horned devil. I was in a struggle over whether or not the doctoral program was something I wanted to continue. There was something missing in the overall program. The missing piece involved the overemphasis on verbal exchange, which is the primary tool used for change in psychoanalysis. I wasn't the only one missing it, there was plenty of discussion going on at the institute, but what was "it"?

"This card shows your destiny is in the body—perhaps that's your Shamanic interest right now." My suspicion was that the psychoanalytic field underemphasized the body. All of that talking, talking, talking—where did the body come in? Did I even know much about the body I carried around with me as a daily requirement for being human? I sure as hell knew a lot about the mind, the psyche, emotions, and beliefs—but, what about my body?

"Ah, sweetie, this card shows that you're going to struggle with this for awhile, another six months or so."

Something cleared the fog inside my mind. "Do you think I'm addicted to the struggle—that the idea of struggling with decisions, and ways to look at the world, feels more productive to me when I agonize over them?"

"It might be a habit—the struggle," she contemplated a moment before she pointed to the next card. "This card shows your success with people—you're a therapist, right? People around you are relieved of their burdens, while you continue to struggle inside of yourself. Oh, but look here, this card shows an interest in health—it's the ace of the suite—a card that shows vibrancy. But it's upside down—you are finding that your health is somehow unattainable." Tears began to roll down my cheeks.

With all of my ability to relieve others of their burdens, I continued to carry around my own.

"The last couple of cards are outcome cards—they show probability—what will likely happen if things continue as they are now."

I looked down at one of the cards to see a woman twirling in a flowing purple gown, her head in the clouds around her.

"It will take some time, but you will make a decision. You need to incorporate the body into your therapy—if you stay solely in psychology you won't be happy. My advice is to finish your program, but to somehow incorporate the body and the mind. Meanwhile, find someone who can teach you about your body."

I went home and within a month's time came into contact with a man who practiced working with Chi Gong, the art of balancing energy in the body through massage. For the next three years we worked together as I learned to get in touch with my own body through energetic bodywork. Not only did I learn about my physical body but also I learned about myself, an energy component of me that had been squelched for many years.

The "self" I needed to lessen in this instance was the emphasis on my thinking process—a thinking process that was inundated with "struggling" as a means of engaging with decision-making. My internal dialogue was so familiar to me that I didn't know it was even occurring. It was the way of thinking that I was most familiar with for any given situation. The Tarot reader suggested I get in touch with the other part of "me" or my body, which had been flattened and smothered by my addictive and familiar manner of thinking and viewing the world.

We're going to go right into another component of self-importance in order to round out the picture being drawn here of what self-importance entails. In order to lessen the "self" it is critical that we take our focus off of ourselves. It is not that we want to focus on others without first knowing our own self; I am not advocating that we become selfless in our attention in order to focus on others. Too many people make service to others more important than service to one's self. They are serving in imbalance because they have not first experienced how to serve themselves thoroughly. Once we can serve ourselves in a healthy way we know how to serve others within balance.

Rather what I am advocating for is that we recognize our place in the larger scheme of the Universe. Too much focus on self or too much focus on others is out of whack with all that is available in this big, unfathomable Universe. Shifting our point of view away from human beings entirely may be what is called for because society's value on human life is skewed to the detriment of all other life forms. Gaining a balance with all that the Universe has to offer will lessen our self-importance.

Early on while walking this path a gentleman suggested I pick up the stone that called to me. I looked down to see hundreds of canyon rock and pebbles and stones strewn along the path we were walking. How in the world was I going to be able to discern which stone was calling to me? Did I look for a stone with pleasing color or one with an unusual shape or blindly reach down and just grab one? Did I sit down and wait for one to stand out from the others and speak with an inner voice that would distinguish itself? How was I going to pick up the very stone that called to me? I was puzzled and frustrated.

The gentleman said not another word but walked alongside me in total silence; not even his footsteps made a sound. I leaned over and picked up a stone. And, without thought, suddenly I knew: when I picked up the stone it was due to the very fact that the stone had already spoken to me. The action of bending down and reaching for a stone indicated I was the responder in the encounter and not the initiator. Whether or not I heard a voice, saw a sparkle, or liked the shape of the stone was irrelevant. Simply the action of bending down indicated the connection. What I needed to shift was my emphasis on who was important in the interaction. I learned that I am on even ground with the stone. My humanness is not the central figure in the interaction. I learned that things, events, and people come to me that will impact and teach me on this path.

Herein is the message: significant issues of self-importance will come to the warrior/sorcerer to be dealt with. Every one of us feels self-important; it is part and parcel of our socialization. The emphasis is not, "How self-important am I?" but rather, "What action can I take to lessen my self-importance?" What you need to be convinced of is that self-importance permeates our beings and a warrior/sorcerer takes action to lessen it.

Self-importance is the counterpoint of the Toltec concept of awareness. There are many working concepts in the warrior/sorcerer's realm that are the antithesis of those in the everyday world. The simple explanation for this is that humankind has an innate connection to things of the Spirit, but in their endeavor to live life, they have counterfeited those ways of being rather than to return to the original state by remembering that very connection. Self-importance is a pivotal one. Mankind has made substitutions for Spirit for so long he is unaware of the original intent of the body functions conducted by the mind and by our feelings. In the warrior/sorcerers realm, self-importance reigns as the number one imposter. Even though every warrior/sorcerer's self importance will become evident in a manner peculiar to the warrior/sorcerer, the following story may trigger connections to your own self-importance. From there you can begin to Track what needs addressed in your own life.

Bruce, the masseuse that taught me energy work, began this morning's bodywork at my sacrum. Long before I was able to relay to him where tension might be held in my body, he could easily read my energy. This morning tension seemed to be located toward the base of my spine. As his hands molded themselves along the curve of my back, I felt the urge to kick. Immediately, a wave of affect washed over me. I felt sadness, irritation, and anger. My leg twitched, almost violently, banging against the massage table again and again.

"Dangerous." The word traveled across my mental screen. I told Bruce.

"Really, that's interesting." He removed his hands from me. "Right when you said that, I could hardly hold on anymore. It was like I was in a hurricane; I was drained of energy. Let's have you rollover." Slowly, I rolled over.

"Go ahead and kick," Bruce gently encouraged me to allow the movement of my leg which he couldn't help but notice as it twitched in spasms as I lay face down on the table.

Immediately, my mind went into action. "You don't really want to do that, do you? You would look foolish. Look! The urge has passed; there's really no need."

Bruce continued to encourage. "It seems as though you never really got the opportunity to throw a temper tantrum. Why don't you allow yourself to do that now?" He began to work on my shoulders as my legs began to move once more of their own volition.

An image filled my mind. It was the image from a decorative plate in my living room. On the plate a beautiful little girl is seated at a piano. She wears a robin's egg blue dress. Her mouth is open in song; her fingers are pressed on the piano keys. There is a single red rose in a vase placed on the piano. I told Bruce about the image.

"I don't even play the piano or sing," I said bitterly. "I hate that little girl! I could kill her!" My eyes remained closed, and my heart pounded. Hatred filled the room. Both legs worked furiously on the massage table. The kicking came in waves, at first violently and spontaneous, then rhythmic and consistent. Bruce was pressing hard on a knot in my upper right shoulder. The pain was excruciating. I screamed aloud.

"You know you are the little girl," Bruce quietly announced in the silence that followed my scream. I had no thought; no further images came forth. Suddenly, one leg slammed forcefully into the other leg. Pain radiated all the way down the leg. Tears exploded from my eyes. Without one word from either of us, I knew that I had kicked my leg with a vengeance that was beyond reason.

"I've never seen anyone kick themselves as brutally as you've done. Look at your right leg. It is positioned laterally, out of touch with itself. Look at the left leg. It is turned and curled to the inside, towards the right leg. What feminine part of you wants to hurt the male part of you so?"

My eyes grew large. I began to construct in my head a story line that would explain my actions. Why would such a brutal part of me hurt myself so viciously? (Remember: asking "why" creates blame. I was on my way to adding judgment onto my actions.)

"Be careful, don't create a bogey man out of this. It isn't as big as your mind is going to make of it." Bruce read my mind, intervening quickly. "You are at the open door to something big. You're working with it! We're here—and it will come—but making it into a big huge monster is not what is needed."

For a moment, I became aware of how both the known and the unknown frightened me. At some moment in time past, I had told myself, "You must be a good girl; you must sing and play the piano for that is what good girls do," while at the same time, I knew a part of me that wanted to kill and hurt and maim because I couldn't perform perfectly any longer.

"The little girl doesn't need to be killed, but given what she wants," Bruce suggested.

More tears sprang to my eyes upon hearing Bruce's soft voice. Instantly, I saw through the subterfuge of my thoughts. This was about self-image, and how I had maintained a perfect picture of myself as an obedient child and now, as an obedient adult. But that very image was a devouring monster—always demanding to be acknowledged, to play the piano and sing, yet never actually gaining satisfaction. If even once that little girl were satisfied she would be out of work. She was created to carry on a most important function: to remind me of what was lacking in my self-concept. If I gave myself what that little girl demanded, she would be out of a job—she would cease to exist. She would die. I was a slave to my own self-concept, and that self-concept was a tyrant in the form of a six-year-old little girl playing the piano and singing a song.

Self-importance comes in any form, but it is always demanding, devouring, and distancing. Self-importance demands our time and attention. We think we cannot live without it. It devours whatever we give it; it has a bottomless belly that cannot be satiated. Self-importance distances us from our other self; it knows that the two cannot cohabit within the warrior/sorcerer. Even in the form of a defenseless child seated at a piano, it demands allegiance and devotion.

Worth mentioning are two kissing cousins to self-importance: self-reflection and self-pity. They are at two ends of a continuum and are deeply embedded in the social matrix. First, there is self-reflection. Although self-reflection has been around in the dynamics of politics, philosophy, and religion for thousands of years, the newest paradigm to promote its tenants is psychology. By itself it may only be a facelift on religion, but due to its success in the Western world, psychology has taken on a life of its own. Psychology prompts an understanding and assessment of the "self" by putting on a pedestal the study and science of all that pertains to the person's "self". We have an entire industry of self-help: human services. It is not that this complex social machine doesn't aim for good, to stop at that evaluation would be missing the point, but what it does do for many human beings is to distract from any further journey into the mystery of human perception and capability. It proclaims to be both the journey and the destination. (To be fair: transpersonal psychology delved into the connection between the self and Spirit upon realizing that the correlation between the two was missed.)

Let's not throw out the baby with the bath water, though. It is a healing experience to go on a journey to discover aspects about our selves that tend to thwart growth and abundance, but herein lays a potential quagmire of self-important functioning. It is all too easy to get waylaid by the vicissitudes and details of exploring this self, which the Twentieth-century psychologists have created. Our self-importance, and hence our self-reflection, much of it embedded in our idea of "self", is a hindrance and waylays the warrior/sorcerer on her journey to freedom. The trap that self-reflection within the realm of psychology sets up is to become enamored with detail and depth in regards to practice. Psychology as a field has developed a paradigm of thought that runs the risk of becoming dogma and ritual ad infinitum. The balancing act is to use psychology as the tool that can address areas of concern and then move on.

Psychology has been made the culprit in regards to self-reflection, however it is not singularly guilty. Let's broaden the picture. Self-reflection can be found in any and all endeavors that man attends to, including but not limited to: arts, sciences, humanities, politics, philosophies, and religions. The reason self-reflection is not partial is because man is self-reflective regardless of the focus of the reflection. At its very base, self-reflection is a defense; and as curious as it may sound, it is a defense against freedom. Mankind is comfortable with the egocentric study of his own species and those species closest to him. If man metaphorically lived in a box throughout his lifetime he would be comfortable with the perimeter and contents of his own self-imposed limits. Self-reflection is perceived to be a worthwhile endeavor inside these parameters. For the warrior/sorcerer, self-reflection is a trap exactly because it keeps her in that box. She cannot attend to anything else while her focus is directed on herself.

Oddly, self-pity is the flip side of self-reflection; it is self-reflection gone awry. When man pities himself or others he is victimizing those who are the object of his self-pity. "Pity they cannot do for themselves." "Pity their life is such-and-such." Self-pity paralyzes the recipients; they cannot act while they are feeling such feelings of self-recrimination or self-doubt or self-suffering that keep them in the realm of their own predicament. In contrast, the modus operandi of the warrior/sorcerer is to act. She is not paralyzed nor stultified by anything going on in her life and, if she is, it is temporary because she knows that action is the name of the game. Self-pity is all about "me," and the warrior/sorcerer wants to explore the Other. We'll look more into the Other shortly, but for now, it is mentioned because it is the polar opposite of self-reflection and self-pity. It is the realm of Power and therefore the destination of the warrior/sorcerer. The warrior/sorcerer wants to lessen her self-importance, self-reflection and self-pity because with such an overload of "self" there is no room for Power. The "self," in all of its ramifications, is the antithesis of the Other, and the Other is the training ground for the warrior/sorcerer on her road to freedom.

One more distinction needs to be made while on this topic of self-importance. The context in which self-importance has been placed is usually within the warrior/sorcerer's awareness. Unfortunately, self-importance runs deeper than what we know about ourselves, much deeper. Being able to identify aspects of our personality that need change, or reordering our relationships to reflect our interest in the Toltec journey is a good place to start, but self-importance is a multilayered monster. It runs deeper than these surface concerns. "How deep?" you ask. Remember, we are aiming for perceptual freedom and full awareness of our energetic potential.

If the journey was only about clearing out personality complexities or relationship difficulties the field of psychology could do a decent job, but the warrior/sorcerer is after an altogether different goal. The warrior/sorcerer wants to be largely free of "self" in all of its negative and positive guises. The world of daily reality emphasizes the positive traits of the "self" as a counter balance to the negative, whereas the warrior/sorcerer wants to rid her self of any and all attention lauded the "self." The warrior/sorcerer wants out of the box altogether.

Human beings have an overpowering tendency to pay attention to only one thing at a time. If we are entirely present and focused, that's really all we can do; paying attention to one thing at a time is not a bad thing. But we are not always capable of being entirely present and focused. In other words, we are not always present, but more often than not, we are splintered; we are muddied with multiple foci. In addition, we are locked into focusing on only a limited quantity of perceptual possibilities, hence being caught in the box in the first place. Outside that box there is another world available to us, the Other. It can only be reached by getting outside of the "self." The "self" and the Other are different worlds. In the world of the Other there is no "self"; this is the freedom talked about by the warrior-sorcerer. The depth of our attachment to the "self" is the degree to which we can even entertain the thought that we might be better without it! Even though lessening self-importance may start out about knowing more about ones' "self" so that we can become better balanced in the world, it is infinitely more.

Lessening self-importance is about stepping outside of the "self" to the point of entering a world in which the "self" doesn't figure in at all. The sorcerer's realm is about energy and any amount of self-importance is like trying to mix oil and water. The two substances don't mix; their chemical components keep them forever separate and incompatible.

The more we are involved in our self-importance the less we will be able to access Power. Conversely, the more we gain access to Power the less involved we'll be in our self-importance. The two are diametrically opposed to each other; they are polar opposites of one other. This does not mean that the more a warrior/sorcerer knows of the "self" the less she can know of Power. What it does mean is that the more of the world created by "self" that is inhabited, influenced, and cohabited by the warrior/sorcerer the less energetic capacity she can offer to Power. The warrior/sorcerer must work at freeing herself of self-importance in order to allow the energetic encounter with Power to take place.

The fourth year into the doctoral program I began to question what I was doing. Since entering the program directly from my masters program, I had been convinced of my goal. My momentum was going strong and would carry me through an arduous program in psychoanalysis. Besides, if I was going to spend the rest of my working career in the field of psychotherapy, I wanted to be trained in a field of expertise that I firmly believed had the capability of changing people for the better. Why not go to the core of the human psyche, to the very threshold of human relatedness, and decipher with the client the inner workings from earliest childhood? My own analysis had taught me more about who I believed myself to be than five years of previous psychotherapy, and my own work with clients had reiterated the need for such inner exploration. On top of the desire for specific training, I had challenged myself with getting a doctorate degree. In this day and age, it could only help to have post-graduate work and a title to go along with it.

I wasn't tiring of my non-stop schedule seeing clients, working in foster care as a supervisor, and going to school. No, what was unnerving me was my weekend activities and "recreational" reading. How could reading Carlos Castaneda overturn my view of the world to the point that so much felt contrary? If I was reading accurately, the gist of what he was saying was that we as human beings limit ourselves in a world of unfathomable mystery and wonder due to our self-imposed perceptual handicaps. But really, what did that mean? I was already exploring the inner world of the mind and emotions and, what a vast world it was! The theories and postulations and hypothesis about what made the human mind work were legion in and of themselves.

And what about my clients! Didn't they bear out all of what I was reading and discussing in the classroom? The psychoanalytic world was onto the importance of experience as a learning paradigm; only through the analyst's own analysis and work with private clients in analysis could I earn my doctorate in the end. I loved the challenge, the knowledge, and the experience! But something was beginning to erode that devotion. Reading the stories told by an archeologist forty years ago who had dominated the New York Times Best Seller *list were beginning to put a dent in my devotion to the study of psychoanalysis. I began to experiment with what Castaneda was proposing—on the weekends only—after all I was busy and engaged with my life's work studying the psyches of people lying on my couch.*

One year later, I left that doctoral program. I discovered that the psychoanalytic world trapped people in their own words, had little bearing on body awareness and knowledge, and narrowed healing to the significance of past memories. Or, to put it more directly, I was trapped in words, I was not honoring my body, and I was focused on the past, an energetic anomaly. All of this self-importance had squeezed from my life the mystery of the Other, the mystery of my contact with Spirit and Power and energy, all of those things behind the stories of Carlos Castaneda. Leaving the doctoral program was not an easy decision—never had I realized how attached I was to a set of beliefs and experiences! I was full of words that profit so little in the end! I was finally ready to set aside those aspirations of self-importance and get on with my newly emerging involvement with Power.

Chapter 3 Workout:

1. Identify an aspect of self-importance that came to mind for you as you read this chapter. What action can you take to lessen your self-importance?

2. How are you a slave to your own self-concept?

3. What do you pay attention to in your life? Is Power present? If not, go after it. This may mean that you need to stop paying attention to whatever it is that keeps Power at bay. You want Power to be present in order to engage with it!

4. Begin to differentiate between the two "selves" that form who you are. When does each one of these selves show up in your life? What can you do to give your self more freedom?

4.

A Different Language

The house is vaguely familiar. I know the layout and proceed down the hallway that opens onto a large, breezy, sunlit entryway. The double doors are painted white and have leaded glass inlays that allow even more sunlight through their clear, beveled curves. I feel lighthearted and carefree as I casually enter the area. Ahead of me in the center of the white, tiled floor is an oversized crow. Not only does an exceptionally large crow stand in the tiled entry, but also the crow has gauze covering its eyes. I smile in anticipation of our conversation, feeling certain that I will find out what the crow's visit is all about, including the bandaged eyes. I take a confident step forward. With a characteristic crow hop, the bird turns away from me and exits the front doors. My mouth drops.

"What? We're not going to talk?" I question as I waken from the dream. Long association with Crow convinced me that this crow was an omen; but I had also been convinced that our conversation with each other would identify what the omen was about. The crow had disappeared, but it was now up to me to read the signpost provided by his mysterious appearance.

Omens are the language of Power. Signposts to Spirit, omens are a direct line of communication with the warrior/sorcerer from the very source of our existence. They are unidirectional. The warrior/sorcerer is the recipient of the omen and not the originator. (Although down the road, the warrior/sorcerer recognizes that the Other—an aspect of who she is—originates the omens.) The warrior/sorcerer avails her self of the omen; she uses the omen for the purpose for which it comes and that purpose is to provide direction.

The omen comes from Spirit, imbued with Power, and it is the task of the warrior/sorcerer to translate the omen for the occasion at hand. Omens are unique in the realm of sorcery in that they don't require the same type of vigilance that Power does when it comes as an enemy, when the warrior/sorcerer needs extraordinary caution because an adversary is approaching. The warrior/sorcerer is on her toes to be aware of the omen in the first place, but not necessarily in a fighting stance in order to engage in confrontation with an opponent. Omens are a language providing such a breadth and depth of knowledge that the warrior/sorcerer would do well to make their use an essential tool in her repertoire on this path. They are our prerogative to explore as warrior/sorcerers. Very much like learning a second language, the warrior/sorcerer begins with the basics: learning the identification of simple names and places, and then developing them into the nuances of mood or emotion, intention or motivation, as she practices the art.

Crows were a constant source of confirmation and assurance when I first began engaging with omens. Southern California is home to the large, black, and oftentimes, raucous bird that is also well known in the stories of Carlos Castaneda as he traveled back and forth from Los Angeles to Mexico in his sorcery training with Don Juan Matus, the enigmatic Toltec nagual. The link between the land and the animals inhabiting the land is a rich resource in the realm of omens, a fact that was not overlooked by Castaneda or his mentor, Don Juan. Even though the variety of potential omens is endless for the warrior/sorcerer, it was through the medium of crows that I received innumerable signposts for my beginning journey.

At one time, I was on the road for over two hours each day traveling to and from the agency at which I was employed. Brand new to Toltec ideas and experiences, I wondered how omens really worked. How could an extant object communicate with me on the level of my thoughts and feelings in the moment? It was easy to read stories of Castaneda and Don Juan out on the Sonoran Desert changing their plans for the day due to a crow flying overhead, but what about driving the highways and byways of Southern California, in and out of my vehicle during much of the day, and in and out of homes and offices as a foster care supervisor?

I began to experiment. Driving along I would be in thought about my newest readings or a dream from the night before or a question to pose if I had had a "Don Juan" to ask. I would formulate the question and give a time frame for the "answer" to come. The omen would come in the form of a crow that would fly overhead, directly in my field of vision as I was seated behind the driver's seat of my car. Initially, this seemed a preposterous idea as though it was all contrived by an overactive imagination. Believe me, I have an idea of what you're thinking in this moment! But I had plenty of time to verify its occurrence each day. Out of literally nowhere that I could see, I would pose my question and Boom! —A crow would fly across my field of vision. If you've been in Southern California you might also think, "Not too implausible, after all there are literally millions of crows that inhabit that area!" Initially, I would have agreed with you. But months of experimenting, asking more and more specific questions, watching as either a crow would come or no crow would come, and acting on the information given, and the world of omens opened up.

An interesting correlation occurs as I write this portion: that particular employment position lasted only as long as it took me to grab hold of omens as a viable source of direction. Where else would I have had the time or rather taken the time to experiment over and over with the experience of seeking direction and having an extant event occur simultaneously that supported that knowledge? For me, it was a period of intense training in paying attention to omens and giving them credence as a means of making decisions.

If we go back to our original premise for a moment, we can put omens into proper perspective for the warrior/sorcerer. Power is deadly, but without encountering it, the warrior/sorcerer is powerless to advance her way to freedom. Freedom is evolution to our highest potential in a universe of infinite energy. That concept in itself is so abstract as to be nearly impossible to grasp. How can we grapple with abstract concepts

Encounter with Power

when the daily world is busy with a multitude of things vying for our attention? It's not nearly as impossible as it sounds because we are creatures of vast potential. In that vastness of potentiality we have proven to use very little of the resources we have available at our disposal. Given our potential, therefore, we are capable of taking notice of occurrences outside the norm of what we're accustomed to. Taking notice is what it takes to travel this path.

Power comes as crumbs in the forest leading seekers to the knowledge they seek. In a world filled with distractions and disturbances that hinder all warrior/sorcerer's bid for freedom, omens come as morsels of guidance. All the warrior/sorcerer need do is to avail her self of the signs. When she does, the warrior/sorcerer is exchanging what she perceives to be the concrete for the abstract, one experience at a time.

Let's go back to a stated premise: we live in an energetic universe therefore everything about us is composed of energy. The warrior/sorcerer is learning step by step that there exist only two ways in which to employ energy: we either expand our energy, or we drain our energy. When an omen is noticed and taken as a viable means of making decisions, that warrior/sorcerer is building her personal power to engage more and more with Power in order to challenge Power itself. Sounds simple, right? Then why is there an entire chapter on omens? If they are bits of nourishment dropped along the path to partake of, what more can be said concerning them?

It is not without purpose that this chapter follows the chapter on self-importance. To the warrior/sorcerer self-importance will mute her ability to engage with Power. The two cancel each other out in a manner of speaking; they are antithetical in nature to one another. The same blindness will occur as the warrior/sorcerer begins to use omens, too. Self-importance denies us from viewing the mystery and wonder of the Universe. As we lessen our self-importance we have the energy to engage other worldly adventures, and omens are definitely in this category. The odd juxtaposition between self-importance and omens is this: beginning to engage with omens will help us see our self-importance.

A Different Language

You are driving along in your car pondering the whole idea of omens: Do they work? Will they come to you? How do you know for sure that you aren't making the entire thing up in your mind? You are curious, and with some amount of determination pose a question: "Will an omen come at my beck and call? If omens are real then show me. Let a bird fly across my field of vision in the next three minutes as I drive on this stretch of road." What happens in the next three minutes will be telling. What is the self-talk going on in your mind? How anxiously do you scan the horizon looking for flapping wings? What if a bird shows up at three and a half minutes? What if no bird shows up at all? What are you thinking as you wait the three minutes out?

Here is the nexus of the example: all of these questions are prompted by self-importance! If our self-importance didn't act as judge and jury, we would know beyond any doubt that a bird was going to appear in our line of vision within three minutes. Power promises to reveal itself! That voice inside our minds telling us "such and so" about the world is self-importance! It is the voice of reason and rationality and reaction.

Try it! Give yourself the experience of observing your "self" in action. We start with rudimentarily setting up a situation and hope to catch an omen in the act. A bird does fly across our field of vision. Now what? We have opened the door to the sorcerer's realm. We have vested ourselves if even for a split second in an alternate reality. We have displaced our mind for an instant and are in wonder that the world is such a mystery. We have gained an ounce, a second, and a pinch of personal power. And in all probability, we want more!

Just like a language, omens need to be used and practiced on a regular basis in order to have any proficiency at their use. Omens come in two varieties, if you will, and without engaging them on a consistent basis it is difficult to always grasp them, let alone decipher what they convey. The first example of an omen has been explained and an example given. The second omen comes spontaneously, or at least unsolicited in the moment. In actuality, whatever is occupying your attention oftentimes directly influences the purpose of the omen. This is a matter of attention—where we place our attention will influence what we end up paying attention to.

Encounter with Power

At one time I was an instructor for a major university that caters to working adults returning to complete or to gain further education. Wanting to diversify in class availability and flexibility of teaching times I was scheduled to take a training course in order to teach online. Within a week I would begin my first course with a mentor instructor to look over my shoulder in case I needed any assistance. I was worried—worried about my computer skills. The course material was not what was causing my anxiety. Working for any length of time with the in-and-outs of a computer program was the source of near terror; doubt about my computer capabilities was eating me up.

Driving home one afternoon, I noticed a large truck in front of me making the circular turn off the freeway to a secondary highway. I noticed a large decal on the back of the cabin window: NO PRESSURE. The truck was shiny black and the letters were solid silver. They jumped out at me due to their size. They were nearly ten inches in height. I gazed at them, thinking momentarily that they were certainly large letters, maybe even auspicious. My awareness stayed with them as both of our vehicles followed the curve of the road. I tracked exactly what I'd been thinking the moment I saw the decal as I blinked at the letters shining like chrome, caught as if a rearview mirror from the sun's rays. I couldn't take my eyes from them: NO PRESSURE. Click. It was an omen! I could approach my first online class with absolutely no pressure. All would go smoothly and I need not squander my energy with doubt. I arrived home and on the top border of the monitor screen I taped a message to remind myself throughout the class: NO PRESSURE. All was well and the computer and I got along just fine.

What caused me to know that it was an omen? Over time and with practice the warrior/sorcerer begins to recognize when an omen appears. It is body awareness more than a mind connection. It is subtle but unmistakable. The body "recognizes" the omen more than does the mind, and responds by quickening. Suddenly, there is a flush of heat and rapid heart beat. Thought flies out the window and you simply KNOW.

Over time and with practice the warrior/sorcerer will notice that the body cues diminish. When first working with the language of

A Different Language

omens, they come with a jolt of clarity that is felt in the body. This jolt or quickening is a teaching tool that helps the warrior/sorcerer recognize the omens. It is all too easy to come to depend on the body quickening to determine whether or not what is happening is an omen, or simply a quirk that the warrior/sorcerer wants to be the omen. It is also the case that the more one wants omens the less they seem to appear. (What is it about wanting something that keeps it always out of reach?) Why would there even be any confusion? Because there are a million decisions to be made by a warrior/sorcerer in the course of a lifetime and depending on the amount of personal power the warrior/sorcerer can claim, those decisions are made either with assistance or without assistance from the ether energy of omens. They are given freely. Avail yourself of this source of knowledge that comes as a guide and mentor to your decision-making.

As the language of omens is developed and practiced, the warrior/sorcerer recognizes that omens also come from within; they are not exclusive to the external, physical world. This knowledge and practice develops over time, too. I wasn't aware of this shift until it happened to me. I was seated at the computer writing. It was early Saturday morning, and the sun filtered through the blinds making the alcove I was seated in light up with a golden hue. After eighteen months of living in Hawaii, I felt the island was becoming my home. The place we were renting provided us with plenty of space, unlike the first small duplex we'd landed in upon arriving. I was working on my manuscript consistently and, it too, was feeling warm and inviting. My momentum was steady and the writing was coming along smoothly.

Suddenly, I heard a voice inside my head, "Call Mark." I dismissed the message, as I couldn't immediately identify anyone by that name. The keys continued to click and clack for an hour. Again, "Call Mark" was spoken. I paused. "Mark is my real estate agent in California." I put the name with the face and paused. It was not my mind that had spoken. The only reason to contact a real estate agent in California related in any way to me was to do something with the place I owned there. For several months now I had been pondering whether or not to buy a home in Hawaii. Was now the time to sell my place in California in order to buy a home in Hawaii? Without hesitation I telephoned Mark. The voice had clearly not been mine and had clearly been an omen. Within two weeks the place sold the first day on the market for over the asking price. I have learned to take action on omens such as this one, which leads us to another critical piece of the language of omens.

Act on the omen. Take the direction the omen is leading you. Make the decision that is pending. Leave doubt behind. Trust the omen. If the warrior/sorcerer doubts the omen and their potency in assisting decision making, she cripples her ability to make use of this form of direction. Omens build on personal power, empowering the warrior/sorcerer to move forward and make decisions she might otherwise not encounter. Again, this is not as easy as it sounds. The warrior/sorcerer begins to distinguish self-importance from the designs of Spirit. This abstract way of being runs counter to our sense of reason, but the warrior/sorcerer knows that omens are not of this world. They are abstract messages that work with symbols, signs, colors, numbers, moods, voices, animals, and actions that often come in odd or extraordinary ways. If they came in an ordinary way the warrior/sorcerer might easily miss or overlook them.

Imagine you are experimenting with working with omens. You "set up" an omen, say for example, "I want direction as to whether or not to speak with my supervisor regarding a change in my job responsibilities." You specify a time frame: within the next forty-eight hours. After lunch on the first day you notice a message on your cell phone asking you to contact the supervisor; you return the call and while on the phone with her/him you take the opportunity to ask if you might schedule time together in order to talk about your present responsibilities. Easy. A time is scheduled and you feel confident that the omen was clear.

Now another scenario: imagine that you are terribly unhappy with your present employment. But you have no clear direction as to how or when to change your situation, whether to move into another field, or whether or not your present employment is not an important learning tool. Previously, you have pondered going into massage, but know beforehand that massage is a difficult profession to make a living at, along with being difficult on the body of the masseuse or masseur.

A Different Language

You're on the freeway driving to that place of miserable employment and glance to your left. There in the distance you notice a pyramid, a structure never noticed before. It's a structure of mammoth proportions so it wasn't built overnight or even in the past six months that you've noticed. It stays in your mind for some odd reason as you continue driving. When you arrive home after work a pamphlet is in the mail from a massage school you've contacted. You open the brochure and in the upper left hand corner is the school's logo: a pyramid with a third eye at the apex of the triangle. It appears to beckon you to apply. Instantly you remember the pyramid on the drive to work that morning. An omen!

You call the massage school to get more detail, all the while wondering how in the world you can attend massage school and work the hours you do. Life is a mystery, you know, but this omen has the potential to send you in directions that will upend your world. Do you pursue it?

The gist of the story is this: omens are intended for more than merely deciding the evening's dinner menu. Omens have the potential to be life changing, and because of this they challenge the warrior/sorcerer's willingness and availability to follow their directives. Some people go to a psychic to gain information, some people read Tarot for directives, and some people read their horoscopes for advice. How many, though, will act on what they are told, or act on what they read? The warrior/sorcerer knows that omens are the language of the Toltec and she pursues them in an effort to stay in contact with the Spirit. In this way she moves forward in her quest for freedom and in her interaction with Power.

Like any language that is spoken, omens are universal to the population that "speaks" the language; in other words, every warrior/sorcerer can "speak" the language of omens. But remember, omens are individual in nature. Not every omen communicated by object, color, sound, mood, or dream will have precisely the same significance for every warrior/sorcerer. In other words, not every warrior/sorcerer will commune with crows! At the same time, each and every warrior/sorcerer will find that the language of omens will develop in tune with their individual bent as a warrior/sorcerer.

Encounter with Power

The meditation was nearly over. I lay on the carpet with my eyes closed listening to the sound of the drum in the center of the circle. This circle of women was new to me since I had moved to Hawaii to study with them only months before. Here I was where my Dreaming had led me, yet I was uncertain. Many changes in my life in the past six months had left me feeling tired. More than physical exhaustion, I was feeling a sense of ennui, a feeling that left me depleted and in dire need of replenishment for my spirit. Suddenly, flying into my peripheral vision from the open window was a crow. He landed next to me and began hopping up and down on the carpet the full length of my prone body. "What is it?" I asked him. I was thrilled to see Crow, as he had been absent since my move. "Stay here awhile. It is a good place for you to be." Before I could elicit any more information, the crow lifted his wings and exited the room. Immediately my concern over my whereabouts eased—Crow had never misdirected me but instead had always provided me with direction and knowledge of where to be on the path.

Crows have been a consistent source of communication for me as I mentioned earlier. They have flown into and out of rooms, flown overhead on freeways and parking lots, hopped onto lawns and buildings in front of me, shown up in mass and as single communicants, and spoken telepathically. They have also changed appearances. Once while Dreaming, two Crows moved by me wearing skates, while at the same time appearing with eye infections that caused their sight to be hindered. Another time a Crow appeared with feathers sticking straight out from his body as though he'd been frightened and had the equivalent of "chicken skin" all over his body. That one wasn't difficult to decipher: in the moment I had been acting like a "scared crow!" Always, they have willingly communicated, whether telepathically or symbolically. As my contact with them increased so did my ability to decipher exactly what their presence indicated for me.

I share my experience with crows, not to indicate that every warrior/sorcerer will have the same experience, but to indicate that every warrior/sorcerer will build their own language of omens—a language that will speak specifically to that warrior/sorcerer's needs. This is the intent of omens; they communicate in the most effective manner possible to each and every warrior/sorcerer who turns to them for direction. They will not fail you!

There is one last nuance concerning omens that the warrior/sorcerer would do well to be aware of. It is an odd phenomenon that other warrior/sorcerers have corroborated with me. The purpose for the shift appears to be due to maturation. Initially, omens come loud and clear. Once a warrior/sorcerer places her awareness on the possibility of them occurring, omens appear with a bang. Their appearance is an announcement. Later they come by less dramatic means; nonetheless the astute warrior/sorcerer won't miss them. Their subtlety makes them no less of a pronouncement. It is as though the warrior/sorcerer develops an attunement to Power that causes the appearance of omens to be less necessary. The warrior/sorcerer internalizes the ways and means of Power such that directional markers aren't used with such frequency. With this shift comes a sense of wellbeing and confidence—all is well and life unfolds exactly as intended.

The following tale is from early in my Toltec adventures and not only provides an ending to this chapter on the language of omens, but segues into the next chapter on Power plants. Portions of the tale have been deleted, as the purpose for telling it in the first place is to highlight the Power of the omen rather than the details of the journey as a whole. Each and every warrior/sorcerer will gather her own tales of power experienced with her own tools of Power. It is my intent to share this tale, not with an emphasis on the use of hallucinogens, but for the manner in which Power comes to guide and to teach the warrior/sorcerer who seeks.

It had been a year since I was last at Joshua Tree National Park and the same amount of time since I last went on a mushroom journey. It is 11:00 am on a Sunday morning and the sky looks heavy with thunderclouds toward the southwest as I drive along the two-lane road heading toward a familiar grouping of rocks inside the park. I wonder how long it will be before those steel gray thunderheads will dump their load onto the desert chaparral. I wonder what I'm doing here and for what purpose. A ceremony will help me decide whether or not to ingest the mushrooms in my pocket or to simply walk the

Encounter with Power

desert until the rain comes. Either way, I am here because I feel drawn to this place, drawn to seek solitude, drawn to gain clarity about my path with heart.

"A path with heart"—what a phrase! Don't I already have a path with heart as a psychotherapist, or a path with heart as a masseuse? Aren't those occupations enough to provide me with an avenue to serve others in addition to an income for myself? Why then does performing those two occupations not satisfy? Seems to me if they were my paths with heart I wouldn't be here, wandering the desert in search of an answer. Climbing onto a large rock, the size and color of an elephant, I burn copal, carefully shielding the rising smoke from the gusts of wind traveling in spent-cartridge circles around me. I pull the eagle feather from my pouch and brush my aura with the copal smoke. It is sweet and soothing and gets quickly carried away by the urgency of the desert wind. The mushrooms call once more and I put them in my mouth without thought. It is decided then. My intention is to discover my path with heart.

I look toward the southeast horizon. In the distance, perhaps a mile or so, I can see an outcropping of rock the size of a small town. Using it as a direction marker to head toward, I start walking while first glancing back and eyeing the marker used to identify the direction of my car in the opposite direction. The desert is deceiving. I have hiked in this area before; I know distance provides distortion and a rock formation close up looks entirely different from several miles away. Lighting changes dramatically, too, as the day wanes, even with the heavy clouds obscuring the sun's rays.

I'm pondering how I set "markers" in my life that provide me with a measure of movement and progress when suddenly the odd thought occurs, "It's happened again. How did I get here? Here, in the middle of the desert on a mushroom journey?" Yes, I had thought about doing the mushroom journey. Yes, I had driven out to Joshua Tree National Park. Yes, I had set an intention, but suddenly, those events seemed orchestrated by "other than me." Those events that led me to be where I was hiking in the middle of the desert, opening the door to the "other world" by lieu of hallucinogens, searching for Spirit, and asking for purpose in my life, were all "directed" by "other than me."

I hesitate to use the word "directed" because that feels like I was doing something aided by something or someone from the outside and it doesn't feel quite like that when it occurs. It feels more like there is a part of me acting that is unfamiliar with being given that choice; a part of me that can direct in a purposeful and meaningful manner on my behalf that I am not entirely familiar with. It feels as though my cognition is in the back seat and this part of me, "other than me," takes over and acts with a clear sense of purpose and direction. (Early on in my travels I was aware of the Other—I simply didn't know it by name.)

Several hours later, I begin to head back toward one of my land markers in order to reach the car. I have over an hour to walk and the sky is truly looking ominous, building and building in intensity much like the sky in Alabama during a lightening storm when I was eleven years old. I can hear the roll of thunder in the distance and, if even possible, the sky is growing darker and blacker by the minute. I smell the peculiar odor of a pregnant storm, that odor that at once smells of electricity and pungent earth just before the storm crowns and birth takes place. Pausing for a moment, I raise my hand in a gesture of challenge, almost inquisition to the Power present.

"What is my path with heart?" What is the activity in my life that I will be best at performing? I know it isn't as a psychotherapist or a body worker. Those are paths that were meant to heal, not only myself but also others I have worked with in the past ten years. I cry aloud, "What is it?" It is not quite a demand; I can hear the boldness in my question without it being a mandate that comes from arrogance. I am aware of the Power in my request. I continue to walk. When are the words spoken that my path with heart is as a writer? I'm not sure. I know that as I walk along I am certain that writing is my path with heart. I smile. Earlier, I had also known that the answer was inside of me, not in the mushrooms, not in the desert, not in the storm but inside of me.

"An omen, give me an omen, to seal the deal," I make my request boldly. Uncle (the Lakota medicine man who watched over my vision quest six months previous) says, "Ask. Ask the Universe for what you want." Unabashed, I speak the words aloud. I walk further and glance at the distance yet to go in order to reach the car. Out of the corner of my eye, I catch an unusual color for this dusty brown and oregano desert terrain. It is a triangle shaped stone, a black and white mottled arrowhead. Catching my breath in awe, I lean over and pick it up. An omen! A lucky stone given by Power to confirm my path with heart now lies in my palm as I continue walking to my car and ponder aloud this Toltec path.

Chapter 4 Workout:

1. Ask (yourself) for an omen today. Set up the parameters: will seeing three orange trucks on the way to work indicate a "yes" related to your question? Will seeing an animal in an odd spot indicate for you to wait? Will a green light within the next mile on the road indicate for you to move forward?

2. What omen have you acted on recently?

3. Begin to identify your "language" of omens. Watch for recurring symbols, signs, objects, and colors that you like or dislike (I shudder when I see too much of the color lavender in a brief time span!) These markers specific to you will begin to help identify your personal language of omens.

4. What is your body's response to an omen?

5. Identify a time when an omen has come to you as a still, quiet voice—a voice inside your head that was not your own. Did you follow the directives of the omen?

5.

Power Plants

As I walked through a forest full of trees reminiscent of the California Redwoods, I discovered that climbing them was quite effortless. Reaching above my head, I could easily swing my body onto a limb and reach for another. Climbing up, up and up, I became aware of the formation of the tree changing as I moved along. The tree had mutated into a gigantic column as I climbed. At the very tip-top there was a room. Feeling a bit of vertigo as I looked way down at the vast distance I had come, I dropped onto my knees in an effort to calm myself. Steadying myself for a moment, I finally turned and walked over to the door. I entered the small room to find a group of people inside who were passing around a variety of plants and herbs.

Apparently their interest was in introducing those new in the group to their wares.

Everyone was friendly. The ambiance was warm and inviting; the color of clothing and baskets, seating and even the flooring was vibrant, each color pulsating with the breath of life. I sat for a long time immersed in the feelings of wonder and curiosity and pleasure; I was unconcerned that I was in an unknown place and with unknown people.

So alluring was the room, the people in it and their wares that I returned for a second visit. This time I knew the routine: make a decision as to what plant or herb I wanted to ingest and it would be provided. I noticed a table arrayed with dozens of balloon shaped containers. I knew they were mixtures of various plants and herbs for the user familiar with their peculiar use. Giggling,

I thought of the popular term from a decade ago, "Designer drugs." Which one would I choose? Just as I was ready to make my decision a call came from below. "Return, for you are needed down here." I was being summoned to care for young ones on the ground, those whose care had become my responsibility.

The only way to get down from the tree column was to drop off the edge of the platform and into the empty sky. I had not noticed before how high the room sat in the atmosphere and how precariously it was perched on top of its swaying column. No problem; I dropped myself over the edge and raised my arms as my body plummeted.

The trick, I knew, was to gain a head wind while at the same time position my arms like wings perpendicular to my body. Making sure that I was holding my arms at just the right angle but without looking down, I didn't notice the tug at first. But quickly the drag was apparent and I looked about me. My wrist had gotten caught in a circular parapet from the roof of the room (the weight of my fall having stretched the parapet to accommodate the distance I'd fallen—dreams are peculiar, aren't they?) Unless I could release my wrist quickly I would be in danger of missing a draft high enough in altitude to navigate my flight. Twisting my wrist in both directions and pulling at the piece of parapet at the same time, I strained, aware I was losing precious altitude with each passing moment.

Suddenly, my wrist popped out of its wooden handcuff. I veered away from the parapet and stretched my arms wide. Catching a wind tunnel not a second too late, I slowed down. The draft was strong and supported my weight smoothly. Dipping and turning, a human gull playing in the salty wind, with air flowing over my body with a sensuousness that told me why birds fly, I swooped once more. The support from the wind rippling along the length of my body was invigorating and caused the fear at my near mishap to evaporate. Effortlessly, I guided my body toward the ground and landed with a hop. The cuffed hand had been a scary moment, unanticipated in truth, but it was over and I was ready for what was to next unfold.

Power plants are teachers. They teach how to shift our perception away from our usual cohesion in this world to one outside of this world. They are unerring in their accuracy and ability to bring about the fluidity needed to explore new realms. They can act as mentor and guide during these journeys into the unknown. To get outside of this world and into another is the hallmark of a warrior/sorcerer. Power plants facilitate this shift to a powerful degree and, at times, more intensely than other means of going about doing the same thing. They open the warrior/sorcerer to gnosis from a position in our consciousness, wherein mankind has the capability to discern the very essence of things.

Power plants can be either subtle or earth shattering in their impact. They can speak so softly as to feel like a goose down feather brushed against a cheek. At other times they do the opposite, by causing buckles and ripples within our being that truly rival the upheaval caused by an earthquake. In either mode, they are relentless in their ability to turn our world upside down. This knack that Power plants have for meeting the warrior/sorcerer at the most advantageous spot for growth is part of their mystery; a mystery that the warrior/sorcerer uses to her advantage as she learns how to access Power from her experience with them.

The gifts that Power plants have to give can be experienced in one journey with them, or in many. How, when, and where each warrior/sorcerer learns from Power plants is as unique as each and every human being, while at the same time being a common agent to shift our perceptive abilities that have been known to sorcerers for millennia.

Two observations about Power plants will lend direction to this chapter. The first observation is to address the negative reputation that Power plants have in Toltec writings. They are presented in one of three ways. First, the warrior/sorcerer is told they are dangerous hence to be avoided altogether. I can only guess at the rationale for stating this hard and fast rule. When a warning of such magnitude is made it is undoubtedly made based on the abuse of their use! Second, Power plants are mentioned briefly as though their use is tangential to the evolution of a warrior/sorcerer. And, for some warrior/sorcerers this has been the case. Power plants have played only a minimal role in their evolution. Third, a spotlight is focused on the drama Power plants can produce with little more added regarding their intrinsic value. What is the reason for this inequity? The reason is simple: Power plants are dangerous—there is no way around it! Warrior/sorcerer's do one of three things: avoid them, use them in imbalance, or use them with due diligence.

Power plants can be volatile, addictive, and deceptive. But that doesn't mean that they need to be avoided altogether, or that the warrior/sorcerer can't be given tools to determine if and when they will be used. If danger itself were the criteria for avoidance, the warrior/sorcerer would not place herself in any encounter with Power at all! Power is dangerous! There is good reason for shunning something that runs the risk of irreversible harm if poorly handled. Yet, my experience with Power plants has been, simply and literally, life changing. As a warrior/sorcerer, you learn to pick your battles—and Power plants were a battle worth choosing.

The second observation addresses the extreme difficulty in conveying an experience with Power plants. It is not much different than trying to explain a powerful dream that you've had—there's always something that gets lost in translation, right? Oftentimes, what gets lost in translation is the core of the experience itself. There is something that occurs that is illusive and ephemeral, that "something" can be exactly what the warrior/sorcerer is after, but to try to explain the experience oftentimes means a diluting of the experience itself. Theoretically, I know the possibilities that can occur while on a Power plant journey. At the same time, I know what my experiences were while using mushrooms. I will share a little of both so that the theory and the story will come together to inform and to enlighten, but I will leave it to Spirit to take what I share and either make it applicable to you or not. Know that it is easy to tell what Power plants do from a theoretical perspective and difficult to tell what Power plants do from an experiential perspective. By doing both, it is my desire that at the end of the chapter you will have what you need to make a decision about how Power plants may, or may not, impact your evolution as a warrior/sorcerer.

The topic of hallucinogenic use for the warrior/sorcerer is a smoldering one: use, don't use, use a little, use a lot. I want to emphasize from the outset that every warrior/sorcerer will make a decision regarding their use. This is not really any different than making that same decision as a non-warrior/ sorcerer: people make a decision at some point in their lives as to whether or not they are going to use any type of drug that altars their perception. This includes every type of pharmaceutical or street drug known to man. In making this decision, the warrior/sorcerer has an advantage. Spirit will either lead them down the path of Power plants, or will lead them in another direction altogether. If they are led down the path of Power plant use, the difficulty then comes in deciding how much to use them. When does their use serve to expand the perceptual capabilities of the warrior/sorcerer? When does their use become a dependency that acts as a roadblock to gaining Power? Answering these questions can be guideposts for the warrior/sorcerer's decision as to whether to use or not. These are the decisions that will temper and guide the warrior/sorcerer as she travels along with the intent to access Power itself, via the medium of the plants.

Power plants are used to accomplish two things: to altar perceptive abilities and to thrust us into the world of Power. They are particularly adept at being able to accomplish both in the life of the warrior/sorcerer. But this doesn't mean that these two endeavors can't be gained by other means, too. Historically, there are many portals, or doorways, to engage with Power, including fear, hunger, sex, massage, sweat lodge, meditation, and Dreaming. It strikes me as curious that there aren't nearly as many opposing opinions about say, having a sexual encounter to induce an altered perception, as there are about whether or not to ingest hallucinogenic plants for the same experience. Our society is steeped in its sense of sexuality, both with repressive and expressive agendas, but sexuality is not touted nearly as often, even in Toltec literature, as a vehicle for the altering of perception as vocally as that of hallucinogens. Nor is chi gong massage, or the basic physiology of being hungry.

Who has created this dichotomy of opinion? Why isn't this chapter on the virtues or ills of being in a sweat lodge, for example, instead of the use of Power plants for the warrior/sorcerer? Notice that the term "Power" is used in conjunction with the term "plant"—no other doorway into the realm of Power is connected so intimately with Power as that of hallucinogens in the minds of many people, including the warrior/sorcerer. It is this immediacy, the pairing together of the terms "Power" and "plant", in other words, their purpose together as a partnership that focus' our attention. Hallucinogens are used for various reasons by various peoples, but our discussion will highlight their unique relationship to the warrior/sorcerer who is involved in an encounter with Power. Oddly enough, Power plants are one of the few naturally occurring objects that hold so much potential for experiencing Power, and by that, I mean to differentiate between naturally occurring objects and objects that have been imbued with Power by an outside agent.

What is the reason, with so many potential doorways to Power that Power plants are singled out as having such a big, bad reputation, even in the Toltec literature? It may be as obvious as the fact that they are illegal—but, that's begging the question because they aren't illegal everywhere in the world. And, the prohibition against their use can easily come into question when they are used for a purpose that is not specifically recreational; hence there are religious sects that regularly use Power plants in their ceremonies. But from a Toltec perspective there is another reason that transcends these moral and even religious statutes. Power plants are the only doorway into Power that is sentient. They have an energetic awareness that is non-human. The same cannot be said about meditation or massage. When we engage with Power plants in order to shift our perceptive abilities we come into intimate contact with an energy awareness that is foreign to us.

Let's go back to the purpose for all that the warrior/sorcerer does: she wants to gain her freedom, and that freedom comes from her ability to perceive the world in a different manner than she has been raised to believe are her only options. Another way to describe freedom is that the warrior/sorcerer releases her self from the discord of energetic connections made for her, rather than by her. When in contact with energy that is non-human, we don't always know the nature of the energetic connections being made. Because the purpose for these energies in the universe cannot always be determined, or even have cross-purposes to the warrior/sorcerer aiming for freedom, it is in our best interest to tread lightly. It is not always clear as to when our involvement is too much and the Power plant begins to determine our fate for us. At that point, we have capitulated to that foreign energy, and we may not have the Power to back out.

The following occurred long before I could articulate that Power plants are sentient with an awareness of their own but, at the same time, I knew intuitively that something wasn't right; something was imbalanced. A lovely couple that was familiar with the plant facilitated my first experience with ayahausca. They guided a journey for eight people on a blustery fall evening that remains with me as a highpoint of personal change. For me, the change I am talking about went to the cellular level. I know during that full evening with the ayahausca that my journey took me to a core level and shifted who I was, who I am, and who I will be. It was life changing!

I watched this couple for the next few months because there was discussion amongst the group about planning for another journey, but I found myself undecided as to whether or not to join them. I had an uneasy feeling, an ambiguous sense. That first journey had been marked by a catastrophic shift; that feeling alone might lead me to shy away from any other encounter with the plant. But what I was feeling was a different sensation than fear. I watched and listened. Over the next several months a pattern began to emerge that I hadn't observed at first. The couple used ayahausca often, talked about their experiences in a covert manner as though they wanted to hide their involvement with the "Vine", and most importantly from my point of view, gave their allegiance to the plant. To me it appeared as though the relationship was one of dependence. They had abandoned their own ability to discern, to decipher, and to make decisions, in favor of going to the plant and acquiescing to it a role they could have been performing themselves. The balance in their relationship to ayahausca was skewed in favor of allowing the plant greater Power in their lives than they themselves could own.

The Power plant was becoming paramount in their energy expenditures to the exclusion of many other tools that served the same purpose, possibly even to the couple's ability to use their own personal power.

Because Power plants such as the mushroom, datura, peyote, ayahausca, or marijuana build a relationship with the user, for better or for worse that relationship will influence the warrior/sorcerer's experience with them. In forming a relationship with any sentient object we need to be as aware as we're capable of being. And, awareness is more than being conscious; awareness is an act performed by perception. It is using our perceptive capacity to determine our actions. We need to be able to discern the answer to the following questions. "Is the aim of the Power plant to further my quest for freedom?" "How will I determine whether it is, or it isn't?" We go to the Power plants to enter into the realm of Power, but we become involved, at the same time, with a foreign energy we may know nothing about—this is cause for careful consideration.

It is interesting to note that Castaneda didn't form an alliance with datura in the same way he did with the mushroom. He used datura several times but then went on to use the mushrooms multiple times. The reason? He formed an alliance with the mushrooms, and not with datura. Realize that we can no more expect to form a relationship with every Power plant available than we can expect to form a relationship with every person we meet. Nor would we want to! As we go after Power, we need to be discriminating in who and what we involve ourselves with. The warrior/sorcerer is running the risk of putting Power plants in charge of her perceptive capabilities and not be aware of it. There is a unique balance to be gained here, a balance gained from the warrior/sorcerer's individual awareness of who she is in relationship to the Power plant, and where she is in her evolutionary process.

There is a second reason for the bad reputation Power plants have that is critical for the warrior/sorcerer to know about. Power plants do for us what we can do for ourselves. Power plants are used to shift our perceptive abilities and to thrust us into the realm of Power. This act of shifting the way in which we perceive the world is a primary goal of the warrior/sorcerer. The hallucinogens do this superbly. They bypass our ego, all of the activity our minds love to perform, and force the warrior/sorcerer into an unimaginable realm of possibility. They can assist us in perceiving the universe without filters and without bias. The key here is the shift in our perceptions. The Power plant facilitates that shift, but the warrior/sorcerer has the capability of maneuvering that shift without the assistance of the plant. It becomes easy to rely on the Power plant to do what we can do on our own.

The error in our thinking would be akin to learning how to ride a bicycle with training wheels but then leaving the training wheels on because they were such an effective aid in the learning process. At a critical moment a person learns how to ride a bicycle due to an inner sense of balance and an external tool, the training wheels, initially provided this balance. Once that inner balance is achieved, the training wheels become a drawback. They become a hindrance to being able to bicycle more skillfully.

There are road signs to look for in navigating the use or non-use of Power plants. Knowing our expectations for them, listening and watching for omens, allowing for the dictates of Spirit to unfold, and, quite simply, asking ourselves what our intent would be for their use, are all means of gaining direction. My first encounter with Power plants was as a direct result of asking for assistance to launch me onto the Toltec path. I was new to this path and in awe of the stories I was reading of other warrior/sorcerers and their encounters with hallucinogens. I also happened to be married to a fundamentalist minister in a denomination that looked down on the use of any type of substance. Having been in such a stringent religious system for many years, my options for getting a hold of anything, much less knowing how to use anything I might get a hold of, were nil.

At the time, I was a counseling intern at a middle school. It was the supervisor that became my omen. Another of the interns was sharing a story about one of the clients. "She's a twelve-year old girl and when her parents are in a drunken fight this girl does the oddest thing. She goes outside to a tree standing in the front yard and wraps her arms around that tree. Weird, huh?"

Jorge smiled and answered with complete assurance, "She knows the tree will ground her." The interns smiled but their smiles clearly showed they doubted his clinical answer. For me, there was something in the way that Jorge answered that lent intrigue to his supervision. I listened carefully to see if he would reveal more. Six months later, I was seated in his office, seeking answers about the topic of Power plants. Asking such questions sends energetic antennae into the universe. Spirit will respond to this inquiry and indicate whether or not they will become part of your Toltec path.

Knowing our expectations for what Power plants do or don't do can also provide us direction in making a decision about their use. There was a period of time in which I was desperate to have experience with hallucinogenic plants. My desperateness was born of a fear that I couldn't change who I perceived myself to be. Power plants seemed the only avenue by which to break the bonds that I felt my mind held over me. During this period, not once did any form of Power plant come my way. Despite actively seeking them, I couldn't get my hands on anything. My purpose for their use shifted, and a year later, the door flew open. They were everywhere. People were giving them to me unsolicited. We need to be crystal clear about our expectations: what do we want the Power plant to do in our lives? By answering this question, we can either explore deeper or move on to other tools that will aid us in shifting our perception.

There is another difficulty involved in the use of Power plants that is oftentimes generated by our expectations for their use. Sometimes we decide what we want from the experience, and thereby miss what actually happens. My first experience with mushrooms is a prime example. I wanted high-rolling adventure and alternative worlds that would catapult me out of the ordinary one that I knew. My expectations were legion and I didn't even know it. It wasn't until some time after the following experience that I gained an awareness of what had actually occurred.

Jorge was seated directly across from me and spoke with a soft voice, answering my doubts and fears. "The medicine can open a person's perception to realms they've never experienced before and act as a teacher. Unfortunately, I've seen too many kids who take the mushroom and get lost in it because they don't know the proper use. Way too many kids come into my office in a state of fragmentation from using them disrespectfully." I was seated in Jorge's office with a dual purpose: I was hungry to learn about hallucinogens myself, while at the same time, terrified that my daughter was too involved in their use, and lost in one of the vortexes Jorge was talking about.

"Of course, in my position as a psychologist, I don't want to be advocating for drug use as society views it, but I do want to educate on the potential for proper use. I am careful when I talk to the kids who come to see me. I listen for any openness they may have to hear that the medicine can be used in a right way. If I sense they are open, I recommend they read Carlos Castaneda."

For six months, I read the original series of books and then found myself back in Jorge's office. "Teach me about the mushrooms," I implored him. He had agreed to introduce me. Now, here I was again, seated on his couch, accept this time I had ingested the mushrooms he had offered forty-five minutes ago. Disappointment was brewing. This was a hallucinogenic experience? It certainly didn't match what I read in Castaneda's accounts.

"Nothing has happened," I pleaded and confessed, at the same time.

"Let the disappointment go." Jorge placed his eyes on me, his eyes doing what an arm does around a shoulder when giving comfort.

"Let go? I'm disappointed. I can't let go!" I screamed silently, as I sat wordlessly on the couch.

Jorge grasped a book from off the desk and turned to a page with a bookmark.

"May I read this poem to invite the spirits to join us?"

I nodded consent, much more preferring to demand a reason for my lack of experience. Jorge's voice was calming. The poem addressed each direction with respect as though they were personified. I focused on his words. Heat began to crawl up my forearms starting from the crease at my wrists. Feeling a prickle, I glanced down, looking for an object to swipe from off my skin. I glanced quickly at Jorge. Again, his eyes performed as his arms.

"Are you feeling anything?" he asked as though his hand had just rested gently on my shoulder.

"I feel very warm," I responded in innocence, unaware that the shriveled, brown mushrooms were making a second appearance in the room.

"Take a little sip," Jorge offered me a water bottle. "Tell me what you notice." Jorge leaned backward in his chair and placed the book on his desk.

"I think I'll just lay down here, if you don't mind," I stretched out on the couch. The words in my head felt big and clumsy and solid. They no longer felt like a part of me; they felt foreign. They were jostling for position inside the enclosed container of my mind. Like cattle crammed onto a freight carrier in motion, they shifted to gain balance, lowing to each other for recognition and assurance of their safety. I pushed the words aside in order to listen.

Attentively, I put probes out for sound against the backdrop of the bellowing cattle. I heard the soft strings of a violin. I focused my entire attention on the notes. Where were they coming from? They were velvet and melodious. They came from nowhere and everywhere. Soft, sweet, tentative at first, the notes gained in confidence as they rose from off the strings. Carried by the notes, I melted into their rhythm. Ah, the smoothness, as though the notes were mercury encapsulated inside a clear vile fluidly moving up and down when tipped. I lay without moving, not wanting them to end. Several hours later, what seemed a lifetime later, Jorge stood at the back door with me as I reached inside my purse for my car key.

"Call me in the next few days," Jorge spoke softly. "Let the experience settle a bit. It has its own nature and will continue to shift inside of you. Take notice of the changes that will occur. You have entered the right side of yourself. That door will now remain open forever."

My expectations for what Power plants would do almost blinded me to what they actually did in my first experience with the mushrooms. I was entranced by the sound of the violin; it permeated my very being with its ethereal notes. I had no idea whatsoever that what was actually occurring involved my perceptive abilities. My ability to perceive was being exercised with absolutely no interference from anything else in my psyche for the first time in a very long time. Infants have this capability from birth, but slowly, through socialization, the natural capacity for direct perceiving becomes dulled. Society, in general, is unaware that this facility for perceiving even exists. My faculty for perceiving was focused entirely on one event while my mind was silent—this is the key to perceiving! This is Power! But I came out of that moment of pure perception to focus on where the sound was coming from. My mind became active in doing what it loves to do: identify and categorize. On top of that, I was disappointed that I didn't see phantasmagorical colors and objects, and meet weird creatures. I wanted an experience filled with otherworldly events!

The focus for the warrior/sorcerer is in placing our perceptive abilities by choice rather than by habit. It is in becoming aware, but aware beyond the level of perception that we've learned to operate from since childhood. We want to work ourselves back to something we've known how to do all along. The danger comes in getting caught up in the visual, emotional, or physical experience of the journey and going after it repeatedly. Becoming involved in everything that is stimulating in our environment is what we've done and what society has told us to do, for a very long time. But by doing so, the warrior/sorcerer sacrifices the exchange that can take place between her and the Power plant.

There are many stories to tell and to hear about the details of what happens during a hallucinogenic experience. They are fascinating to hear as long as the risk of losing what actually happens is not bypassed. It's as though it is dangerously easy to fall in love with the tool and miss the purpose for its use altogether. Most of us didn't think twice about getting rid of our training wheels from our bicycles once we'd learned how to ride, so it may be difficult to imagine the person that uses them far beyond their intended use. That person eventually cripples their bike riding experience because the longer the training wheels are left on, the more they inhibit the bicycling experience. The training wheels begin to limit movement, speed, and maneuverability by keeping the rider on a virtual monorail, traveling at a monotonous speed.

The use of Power plants runs the risk of doing the same for the warrior sorcerer. It is dangerously easy to fall in love with the images, colors, sensations—all of the "bells and whistles" that hallucinogens provide—rather than to really grasp what is going on. It can even be stated that the images, colors, and sensations are comforting for they act as a barrier to the unknown that lies beyond them, just like the training wheels do. The unknown beyond the bells and whistles is Power! It is where the warrior/sorcerer wants to be. What the warrior/sorcerer wants to develop is the ability to place her awareness on the object of her choice, and to know that doing so is exactly what moving perception is all about. This is the act of sorcery in a nutshell!

There is one last difficulty to be aware of regarding the warrior/sorcerer's use of Power plants. (This exact same difficulty is also encountered during our Dreaming.) The difficulty involves the impossibility of the warrior/sorcerer relaying what happens during the journey. This difficulty then translates into a difficult time expressing accurately what happens during the experience for others to actually benefit from hearing about it. In addition, it is clouded with what the warrior/sorcerer's expectations are for the experience to begin with. It is easy to want those experiences that we read about from others, or to compare our experiences with them. Comparisons are not often helpful when we may find ourselves with something altogether different than what we bargained for. Because we are going into the unknown, the experience is nearly impossible to accurately relay, much less to compare or contrast.

During any kind of experience with altered perception, the person experiencing it ends up in the position of being a translator when they attempt to dictate their experience to others. They are literally taking an experience from another reality and trying to translate it into present reality. It's impossible to do! Yet, even though it is a task of Orwellian proportions, we try it anyway! When others read those experiences, it is the version told by the writer that ends up making an impact on the readers, not necessarily what actually took place. The risk here is in being misdirected and misguided; it can make the difference between getting to our destination or in being frighteningly lost.

Look at my first experience with mushrooms again. In the midst of my journey, I hear heavenly notes that cause my entire body to vibrate with sound. After listening to the notes for time that felt like forever, my mind began to try to identify where the notes were coming from. My mind had been dethroned temporarily due to the shifting of my perceptions, so it moved slowly. I could sense it grasping for meaning: Where does the music come from? What instrument is being played? And, it eventually landed upon an answer: "It's a cricket!" Ah, my mind had translated the ethereal, magical experience into something that was known and understood! But by doing so I was working from a limited database: my mind. Who's to say how anyone else would have translated that same experience or how it would have impacted him or her differently than it did me?

Again, here is the difficulty: we try to convey an experience while using Power plants but our experiences are intercepted at some point in the journey by our minds. When our minds interpret our experience, that experience becomes heavily influenced by the mind of the person sharing the experience. At that point, the experience is no longer exactly what took place but merely one version of what took place. Conveying our journey to anyone else may do him or her more harm than good; the warrior/sorcerer doesn't necessarily evolve by hearing someone else's mind trip. Doing so can set up an inaccurate representation of an encounter with Power. The person using them can only truly experience power plants. Anything apart from having the experience is shortchanging those who read or hear about it.

If there is a benefit to be gained from the use of Power plants, it is that they can be a teacher to us, but only if and when Spirit brings them into the life of the warrior/sorcerer to learn and to evolve by her contact with them. Be aware that they can own you rather than you simply experimenting with them. Trust that it is the encounter with Power that is the challenge for the warrior/sorcerer, rather than a hallucinatory journey that may be mistaken for something it is not.

Paranoia seemed to be present at every journey I went on with Power plants. It was part of the territory, I came to see, but that didn't make it easier to experience or to move through. This morning was no different. I was walking along the beach. The sun was barely up and the surfers were already positioned for the next set of waves swelling far out at sea and rolling imperceptibly toward them. I walked along entreating the sun to warm my chilled bones, unsure whether it was the early cold or the ingested mushrooms that caused the shiver running up and down my spine.

Toward my left near the condominiums perched on the very doorstep of the sandy shore, I noticed a gentleman. He appeared to be watching me, or at least his gaze was on me every time I furtively turned around to see if he was still there. Apart from the surfers out in the water, I was the only other person visible along the beach. I continued walking. My mind wanted to help out with the situation that seemed to be growing in intensity with every step I took. Thinking the best way to do that was to doubt, my mind began to question.

"What was I doing walking along the beach on this mushroom journey? Shouldn't I be elsewhere—but where? I don't know, just not where I was—who was that man who seemed to be following my every step?" Suddenly, a sense of panic overwhelmed me. I dropped to the sand. My hands went into instant motion: kneading, churning, digging, sifting, they worked the paranoia.

"Should I be here? What am I doing? Who is that man? Should I speak to him and find out why he's following me? Am I wrong to be here? Am I respectful of the mushrooms?" Maybe this time the mushrooms would best me and I would end up running down the beach like a raving lunatic seeking to claw the demons from my chest. Maybe I didn't know what the hell I was doing because I had read all of the signs wrong!

My hands worked furiously digging into the sand as salt water seeped into the hole. With every ounce of internal strength I could muster, I faced the fear and paranoia. Quietly, like a diamond tool cutting through mirrored glass, I heard the Other, "You are respectful." I stopped; my hands became still. The voice lent calmness to my tortured mind and body. With a sob of relief, I arose. It wasn't a mistake to be here then.

Looking behind me, I could see the man watching me intently. I turned and began to walk. I walked and walked and walked. No longer could I see the condominiums or the surfers or the parking lot where I'd left my car. Gulls screamed aloud as they fought over a paper bag filled with surprise morsels to fill their gullet. Unconcerned that I walked a yard within reach, they raced at each other in a show of bravado, even aplomb, which would make them the newest recipient of the brown bag treasure.

    I glanced around. There was that gentleman again. He was staying a respectable distance behind me, but sure enough he was still following. When I stopped he would stop. When I resumed walking, he would walk too. I walked the pier. He walked the pier. I walked over to the water fountain and gulped freely. He followed suit. I traced my footsteps backward as I headed the direction I had come hours earlier. He followed, walking in his own footsteps. I watched the man and he watched me. He had a sense of comfort about him now. For a reason I couldn't fathom, he was watching out for me. He was my guide. There were no words between us, but I knew he was a part of my world. Without speaking he had joined my journey, indeed walked me through it, and had ended his vigil watching as I walked the boardwalk to my car.

Chapter 5 Workout:

1. What relationship do you have with Power plants? Has your experience with Power plants been a beneficial or damaging one as it relates to the Toltec Path?

2. When does the use of Power plants serve to expand your perceptual capabilities? When does their use become a dependency? Are you able to recognize the difference in your own life?

3. What is your intent in using Power plants?

4. What do you want the Power plant to do in your life?

6.

Manifesting Power

With my backpack emptied and the sun surrendering itself into the sliver of ocean miles away, I glanced down at the altar of stones. By returning all of the stones and rocks to the beloved canyon I had hiked for the past three years, I was saying good-bye. Over the years I had picked up rocks and stones, here and there in my travels, and it was time to return them in honor of their temporary sojourn with me. Now it was nearly dark and the stones formed an altar in the soft dirt at the top of the canyon grade. I pulled in sweet air from the sagebrush, the dry earthy smell that permeated the hills and hollows of the canyon, and expelled slowly. Now sadness permeated the air around me, smothering the sweet air from a moment earlier. Sprinkling tobacco on the altar, invoking the awareness of the stones as recipients of my deed, I thanked them for their guidance.

Tomorrow morning I would be moving to Hawaii and the good-bye gesture was my last contact with these canyon hills I loved dearly. My home was emptied of its belongings a few days before; all of my belongings had been packed, crated, and shipped to a new home. One last night of sleeping on the air mattress in the empty bedroom and in the morning I would hand the keys to the young couple that would be renting the place.

Early the next morning, earlier than I needed to awaken, I was surprised to feel our cat crawling along my back. Odd! We had given our cat away a week ago amidst crying and tears. We had made the decision not to have her quarantined for the required number of months in order to take her to Hawaii.

The decision didn't make giving her away any easier, even though her new family was obviously as taken with her as we had always been.

"It's not Tawny. It's The Cat," I said groggily, explaining the cat's appearance even though I was not fully awake. The weight of The Cat was greater than before. Neither had The Cat ever actually walked on top of me, always choosing before to walk along the edge of the mattress. This time the weight was so great I had to concentrate in order to draw in air to breathe. Slowly I sucked air in with a concentration I'd not used before to fill my lungs.

For the first time in my experiences with The Cat, I felt as though if I moved at an imperceptible pace, I could maintain the cohesion of the dream. With a minute turn of the head, I opened my left eye. Looming over me, breathing with a heavy, wild breath, was a black panther, his left ear and eye appearing enlarged, merely inches from my eye. My breathing stopped. The panther began to lick its paw. The scratchiness of the tongue pulled across the forepaw over and over. The gentle rhythm of purring filled the bedroom. The Cat remained still, its weight heavy on my ribs as though heavy enough to crack them. I turned to my right. Opening my right eye slowly, I could see the outline of another cat's head at close range. It was the golden face of a young lion. The weight was unbearable. Breathing was labored as the weight of The Cat bore down on me. Without thought, I knew they were witnesses, witness to my good-bye gesture the evening before, witness to my move to Hawaii, witness to my venture into the unknown.

To manifest Power in the life of the warrior/sorcerer is an abstract experience on several different levels. Let's first try to grasp what manifesting Power is, and then explore what those levels are comprised of in the light of the fact that each warrior/sorcerer is unique and her journey is individual, as I've already emphasized. It would be most beneficial to state loudly and clearly another immutable Toltec law in order to put the context of manifesting Power into perspective. The Toltec rule I refer to is the dichotomy between individuality and commonality. We are both unique and non-unique, to state the proposition patently, though rather blandly. Not only is Power manifested uniquely to each warrior/sorcerer but also Power manifests in recognizable and reproducible means to every warrior/sorcerer. Grasping this rule is somewhat like attempting to pinpoint gravity apart from evidence in the concrete. We can see that gravity affects objects, although we cannot separate the objects from the force of gravity itself.

Manifestations of Power occur in every warrior/sorcerer's experience, though no one can definitively state how and in what manner it will manifest. If I say to you, "I cannot tell you how Power will manifest in your life," but then later say, "Power manifested a similar way in my life, too," you may readily point out the discrepancy between those two statements. Not simply a matter of time difference, as in "hindsight is always 20/20," it is more the acknowledgment that Power is a mystery that can evidence earmarks of familiarity across a sample of sorcerers. To state it another way: every warrior/sorcerer manifests Power in an inevitable and recognizable manner even though every warrior/sorcerer is a unique individual. Clear as mud, right? Let's delve into this conundrum as much as is possible because even though it is a slippery notion it is vital for growth.

Power can be manifested in a conscious manner and in an unaware manner. I won't go so far as to say "in an unconscious manner," because what our minds conceive is vastly different than what our bodies, either physically or energetically, can be aware of. In fact, Power has a way of developing and increasing without our awareness for a period of time early in the experiences of a warrior/sorcerer. This makes perfect sense in that we are unaware or unfamiliar with the terrain of a Toltec path when we initially begin to walk the path, and therefore we don't always recognize what may be happening. Our inexperience keeps us from being aware of what will later on be extremely obvious.

As warrior/sorcerers we come to experience external forces that act upon us apart from our relationship to Power. The Other is an example of just such a force. (It can be argued as to whether or not the Other is an internal or external force—for now it is being used as a force operative in the life of the warrior/sorcerer distinct from Power. An argument about the specifics of the Other deserves its own study and does not fit into the present discussion.) Therefore, events occur in our lives without our knowledge and before we are aware of what is actually occurring, relating to the sorcery realm. Again, this sounds blatant, but to observe when situations arise that feel unfamiliar and foreign and yet to grasp those events in the light of Power doesn't always come "naturally" at first. To gain the balance between what we are responsible for creating and what is thrust upon us as we engage in a sentient universe is the art of sorcery.

Bruce lay on the massage table and I began to work on him. It had been some time now since Bruce and I had begun to exchange energy work via massage with each other. Closing my eyes helped me to sense the energy in a deeper way than when my eyes were open and more easily distracted by my surroundings. Bruce was lying face down on the table as I effleurage his legs. The long, light strokes were used at the beginning of the massage to warm the skin and to connect the energy between the body worker and the client lying on the table.

Soon I slowed my strokes and began to connect to where I felt the most potent energy. Bruce had taught me to "go where you feel led." I was not to think about anything but to let my hands lead instead. I began to concentrate on his right calf. As I explored with my eyes closed, Bruce narrated my movements. "That's the meridian to the kidney," or "You're right on the meridian to the spleen, the meridian that runs from the large toe all the way up the body." I was in a wonderland, moving slowly as my fingers picked up his chi in various nodal points within the five-inch radius that was his calf. Slowing down even further, I began to concentrate on a small, one-inch square area. There was absolute stillness in the small room. Bruce lay as though he was a dead man. The only movement was my left hand as it moved at the pace of a seedling breaking through soft soil to reach for the sun. Absolute stillness permeated the room. Even my thoughts were still.

Without warning, my fingers slipped through the skin as though an aperture had suddenly appeared. I could feel my fingers slip and slide through space where a moment before there had been solid matter. My eyes flew open! "Hey, this weird thing just happened!" I explained to Bruce that my fingers had been incisors, cutting through his calf like a scalpel. Bruce replied, "The more you work with energy, the deeper go the depths of the altered state." Dear Bruce knew in the moment something

I was only beginning to decipher: we were dealing with Power as we bypassed the dictates of time and space.

If Power is the fuel that propels us forward along the path, it does so in differing degrees of influence. Manifesting Power allows the warrior/sorcerer to maximize her potential while at the same time maximizing fuel efficiency. Again this is a concept that sounds well and good to read in print, but what does it "look like" in the life of a warrior/sorcerer? Here's an example that we'll look at from two different points of view.

Early in my endeavors with Power plants, I was on a mushroom journey while hiking in the Southern California hills. Anyone familiar with the area would know that poison oak is rampant in the coastal desert, a fact I was well aware of. What I had not figured on was the potency of the mushrooms and the impact they would have on me as I hiked along. At one point, I glanced down, shocked to notice that I was in bracken and bushes that included the familiar three leafed, red-orange vine. Riveted in fear, I remembered the last and only encounter with poison oak that left me with patches on my legs that oozed and itched and radiated pain for weeks.

I stood stock-still. Where to move? Where to go? Without a conscious thought, I gave myself over to my body for permission to take control. Surely, my body had an awareness that my mind did not! My body felt alive and active, as though it could take charge and know exactly where to move. I darted to the left and deftly worked my way up the hill, pushing through low brush and jumping over and around bushes and small trees. I felt like a wild animal, moving swiftly, with complete assurance that I could maneuver the locale. When I topped the hill I found myself on a small dirt road, free of fear and free of further contact with the poison plant. Looking back to that moment of potential when I stood completely frozen in fear, my body manifested Power that my mind didn't have (including the obvious, "Duh, what was I doing there to begin with?") Had I not manifested Power in that moment of surrendering to body knowledge, I can only imagine how the story might have ended.

In that moment I would not have defined my experience as one of manifesting Power. Instead, I defined it as an act of reliance on body awareness. Either definition is technically correct, but with awareness in the moment that the experience was one of manifesting Power, I might have acted differently. To "have an experience" is certainly a goal for the warrior/sorcerer, but to tap into and make use of the forces available in the experience is manifesting Power above and beyond the experience itself. That act of engaging with Power is what the warrior/sorcerer seeks.

Let's put this example into the context of the Toltec law introduced in this chapter. To state the law again: Not only is Power manifested uniquely to each warrior/sorcerer, but also Power manifests in recognizable means to every warrior/sorcerer. If another warrior/sorcerer had been in my predicament, how might Power have manifested? At the moment I gave my body control of the situation, what would anyone observing me have seen? Did I move as though I was a non-human mammal? Would Power have been apparent in my actions, just as gravity is apparent in a falling object? How does the force of Power transfer, translate, and trigger the warrior/sorcerer to act? I suggest that my experience was unique and non-reproducible. Those precise variables could not be set up in exactly the same manner a second time for anyone else. Sure, someone can go into the desert on a journey with Power plants but that wouldn't address the particulars of who I am, the precise shift in my perceptions at the time, coupled with the particular location of my whereabouts.

Surrendering the mind to the body is a common occurrence for the warrior/sorcerer. It is a powerful shift in the perceptions of who we are. Furthermore, I suggest that if another warrior/sorcerer had been observing me they would have recognized that Power was present. Not only would they have seen Power in my actions but also they would have sensed it. Power is a force that can be observed and sensed on an energetic level despite what the eyes see. Every warrior/sorcerer learns to recognize its presence despite the particulars of how it manifests in the physical realm.

The manifestation of Power is when the warrior/sorcerer feels, senses, comprehends, perceives, or evokes the force of Power as present in any given situation. But there is more, so much more! Before we get into what that "more" is comprised of, let's first take a look at a major stumbling block to manifesting Power. The nuance of this action is what initially makes it difficult to observe. It is an automatic reaction to the initial encounter with Power until we take active steps to confront it. Many have been presented with a perceptual image that "shape shifts" depending on how the observer is viewing it. For example, take the well-known black and white picture of a vase. It stands alone, a white object with two handles on either side against a black backdrop. But with a shift in perception the vase becomes the outline of two human faces directly facing one another. The vase disappears from view momentarily; with a slight shift in perception it may return and the two faces then disappear. Initially, the warrior/sorcerer views a situation, an object, even energy, and sees only the vase. They don't think to shift their perception to view anything different. With practice, that image can move back and forth with ease; it can become a fluid encounter with Power. In addition, the automatic reaction to the initial encounter with Power often takes the form of "explaining the experience away."

A friend and I were hiking an area of the island that has in the past held a great deal of Power for me. I go to that spot to connect with Power away from the hectic tempo of everyday living. It was just beyond twilight and we arrived at the top of the old asphalt road at the precise moment when the available light from the evening sky had fled for good. No longer did the shadow of the trees and bushes show against the backdrop of waning daylight. All was in darkness. My eyes searched for any distinction in the dark, but all I could see immediately in front of me was charcoal black. We stood, pausing to catch our breath. A little further on and we would lie out our blanket, lie down, and wait for the stars to show.

Without warning, a woman's high-pitched laugh sounded. It had not come from either one of us. The laughter was friendly and yet held a surrealist quality to it. A laugh that was the Power of that spot; I had heard it before. Grabbing my friend's shoulder I whispered, "It's the spirit of this place." The rush of fear I felt was not an uncommon response to encountering Power. We stood breathless and waited. Sudden movement caused us to pivot and there arising from the low stonewall was a figure.

Seated next to the figure was another person; they arose hand in hand and sauntered down the path.

"Ah, it was the woman, she laughed," my friend defined what had happened for her. She explained where the laughter had come from according to her perception; in other words, she "explained the experience away." I had had a different experience. The Power of that place had welcomed me once again.

Taking active steps to confront our view of the world is what sorcery is about. Using Power as a means of "shape shifting" our view is what propels us along the path. After the warrior/sorcerer begins to recognize Power she also recognizes that it has been building for some time. The warrior/sorcerer does not have to recognize Power as acting upon her life in order for that same Power to have an impact. For my friend who didn't recognize the laughter in the same manner I did, it didn't mean she had no encounter with Power, though to continue to "not see it," or to define it, as something it is not reduces the potential effect it might otherwise have. But if and when any encounter with Power is recognized in body, soul, and spirit, that encounter is maximized fully.

What is the potential effect? What is the "so much more" alluded to above? Think of the term "power" in an ordinary way. Common synonyms for "power" include intrinsicality, potential, immanence, strength, vigor, authority, greatness—all of those ways of being that increase our sense of well-being and completeness. If what we are after is Power in a non-ordinary way, those terms are the tip of the iceberg. Let's use the example of the hike once more. After our engagement with Power, my friend and I continued our hike along the trail. We were looking for a good spot to lie out the blanket to await the coming of the stars. I felt a sense of lightness and listened to myself as I laughed and quipped with my friend. Yet, I wanted to dwell on that moment when the inhuman laughter erupted, freezing us in our tracks. That moment had been electrifying and terrifying in the same instance; in fact, that moment had shifted me into a state of euphoria. I recognized the feeling, the feeling of aliveness, of awareness, of freedom from everyday entrapments. I felt literally light-hearted as though I could lift from the earth and fly into the stars that were beginning to twinkle above me. One second of an encounter with Power and this was the result? It is easy to want more, easy to want to increase the encounters, and easier still to seek out more Power. Roll all of the common synonyms for power into one and the warrior/sorcerer is merely getting close to the actual experience of an encounter with Power itself.

To dwell on a moment of Power and to be able to sustain that moment is a goal for the warrior/sorcerer. Power is present all around us and seeks ways in which to encounter us. Stating it that way, however, needs a cautionary note. It is easy to anthropomorphize Power and we want to guard ourselves from doing that. When we view Power through humanizing eyes we begin to act as though we can influence, persuade, and impact it through our own human efforts. It cannot be done! This too is a mystery because as the warrior/sorcerer grows and matures and evolves, she does begin to wield Power as though it is a tool for use. It begins to appear as though Power is at the command of the warrior/sorcerer.

How can it be one and the same thing? How can we approach Power as the force that it is without automatically trying to relate to it in human terms? If the experience can be described in the following manner it might be clearer to the reader. Power comes initially as an unfamiliar experience, something the warrior/sorcerer feels is foreign to who they are. Slowly, the warrior/sorcerer begins to recognize Power, and to endeavor to sustain contact with it. If I had known while working on Bruce's calf that I could enter his calf to explore the depths of his energy being, I would not have exclaimed loudly my wonder but would have instead continued to explore the mystery. The warrior/sorcerer wants to increase her involvement with any form of Power available. Inevitably, a battle with Power ensues and it is here that the encounter takes place. That moment will determine whether or not further encounters with Power will take place forever after. If the warrior/sorcerer is victorious, it is then and only then, that the warrior/sorcerer imbues Power from within. It is who she is—let me say it again—Power is who the warrior sorcerer is, it is her inheritance, but only after she has fought and won the battle does she step into that inheritance.

The reason then to caution against anthropomorphizing Power directly relates to where we are on the path. If, as a warrior/sorcerer, you are reading this nodding your head in agreement, there is a good chance you have encountered Power, sustained your contact with it, battled, and Power now resides in you. But if you are reading along with a furrowed brow and uncertain about whether or not you have ever encountered Power, the cautionary note is for you. Power is an enemy, yet it is not, and this is a mystery that every warrior/sorcerer encounters. For now the task is to sustain interaction with Power for long enough to learn from it.

I have been speaking within the context of time. "Sustaining" our encounter with Power certainly sounds time related. Because we speak within the syntax of time we use terms such as moments, minutes, hours, and days in order to describe our contact with Power. This can easily become a critical mistake in our thinking. From there we can too easily make the assumption that our contact with Power is valued as it increases in increments of time. More is better, right? That's what "sustaining" means, right? Not necessarily. Power acts outside of time. Our human conditioning and belief about time and space do not impact Power. My most powerful encounters with Power have only lasted a few seconds on a clock once I returned to daily reality, and yet I have been unpacking those moments for years! It wasn't the experience itself that needs to be conveyed but the fact that whatever happened during those moments continues to impact me due to the wealth and mystery of the impact itself. Time was of no relevance. That doesn't mean that the warrior/sorcerer cannot put her self in position to have as many encounters with Power that she can. We definitely want to encounter Power; what we don't want to do is to place value on the length of time in which the encounter takes place.

One means of encountering and sustaining Power is through Dreaming. Dreaming will take you into realms of available Power, therefore it is worth taking up the task of learning how to Dream. Placing your attention onto your dreaming is enough to get you started. You'll notice that the word "dreaming" was not capitalized in that past sentence. Much of what occurs during the night is either dreaming or Dreaming, at least initially. The lower case dreaming is what we do with run-off tension during the day; it is a function of the conscious mind about which volumes have been written in literature, psychology, metaphysics, and even religion. Dreaming for the warrior/sorcerer is something altogether different. It is experiencing other worlds, peoples, and energies that are not available while not Dreaming.

A good starting point for Dreaming is being lucid, that experience of being aware that one is Dreaming and the option of volition at that moment of awareness. As the warrior/sorcerer develops her Dreaming, the opportunity for making multiple choices while Dreaming exists. Dreaming includes having the awareness that one is Dreaming all the way to the choice to leave this world and enter another one altogether. If stories can be believed—and they can—there are tales of warrior/sorcerers making this very choice and never returning to the world we know! The art of Dreaming is a work of significant undertaking and at every step of the way the warrior/sorcerer is building Power. As the warrior/sorcerer experiments with Dreaming she is also experimenting with sustaining her interaction with Power. Sustaining this encounter is the goal, for Power will teach us inconceivable knowledge. This paragraph does little justice to the whole topic of Dreaming. It is like saying, "Freud is responsible for bringing the unconscious into the field of psychology and furthermore, for creating the field of psychoanalysis" while in reality he wrote volumes on those two subjects. Much has been written about Dreaming. But our focus for this chapter has been on manifesting and sustaining Power, and the tease that this little paragraph on Dreaming has been will incite those who desire it to seek more.

Tracking is the other task available to the warrior/sorcerer as a means of manifesting and sustaining Power. Since Tracking involves becoming more aware of and making choices about our behavior, it is the tool we use that differentiates energy enhancing actions from energy depleting actions. At every turn we are called upon to take action, whether it is social, psychological, spiritual, or energetic action. Actually, energy is the primary ingredient in all of those endeavors, but it is easy to differentiate our actions through the lens of various disciplines. Recall my involvement in a doctoral program for psychoanalysis. I entered the program direct from a masters program in counseling; I was indeed on my way to bedding down in the familial bed of psychology.

Halfway through this period of time I began to live as a warrior/sorcerer. As a result, it was during this same period that I determined that the field of psychoanalysis took more energy to engage with than it gave in return. For me it was an energy-depleting endeavor. Easy enough to come to such a decision mentally but the impact on my endeavors was vast. It took six months of untangling beliefs and expectations and assumptions about my investments into the field for me to pull out. I was not only attending doctoral classes, but I was in my own analysis and also seeing clients in analysis. All of these endeavors included financial give and take; it was not only my livelihood, but I was investing in my education as well.

To pull out of those endeavors wasn't easy. I found out how attached I was to those ways of viewing life. The entire period of time I Tracked: I Tracked decisions, actions, patterns of behavior, and patterns of thought. At every turn of the road, I made decisions that produced changes within and therefore changes without. Throughout that period, I gained in my capacity to recognize those decisions that built my personal power and those decisions that were based on values I no longer wanted to support. By freeing up my time and energy, I opened the door to manifesting Power in ways that had been inconceivable before. Even the act of leaving the doctoral program had not been in my realm of possibilities before beginning to live as a warrior/sorcerer!

I lay on the bed early in the morning completely at rest. Suddenly, The Cat appeared! Even though I lay on my stomach with my head turned to the left I sensed, rather than saw, the movement as The Cat walked along the top sheet. Slowly, with purpose beyond daily reality, if it can be described in that manner, The Cat walked along the edge of the bed. It didn't have a conscious awareness, because it wouldn't care, that it was walking along my bed sheets. The accoutrements of the moment were inconsequential. The weight was real, not more real than it had been in the past, but heavier than it had ever been. The Cat was getting large! Coming to the head of the bed where my head lay on the pillow, The Cat prepared to lie down. I didn't see this with my eyes but my body knew. Slower still, the cat lowered its massive body on top of my head. Simultaneously, I could feel the weight and the whiskers of the great cat as it turned to look down at me. The whiskers tickled my face and for the first time the odor of wildcat enveloped me as the breath left its body. Sucking the odor in, I could feel panic coming on. The weight was unbearable; the odor was stifling!

Intoxicated with the power of The Cat, I lay, feeling my body as alive. It had awareness and its own purpose and it had nothing to do with my mind. It was as though a scale weighted with mind and body had finally been balanced when before all of the goods were on the side of mind. I concentrated on breathing through the heaviness of the wild cat in order not to become overwhelmed. Fear arrived and I struggled fiercely to let it be. "Fear is natural; let it go through you! Don't get stuck at fear."

And then I did something that had not happened in the past despite all of my encounters with The Cat. I spoke to it!

"Thank you for coming! Don't let my fear drive you away! I want you here!" The imperatives were loud, not in the least muffled for not speaking them with my mouth. I knew dream communication was telepathic. A powerful, seductive thought then entered my very being. It was as though the desire of it was stronger than I could hold back. The moment it came I had to speak it aloud or else it would overwhelm me with an avalanche of longing more than I had strength to stop. It would flatten me with the weight of its largeness. Without hesitation, and with total surrender of my body, mind, and spirit, I spoke, "I will worship you forever!"

I had my wits about me enough to notice that The Cat did not speak to me. Taking what looked to be golden calipers, a three pronged instrument rather than double pronged, The Cat aimed it at my head. A delicate instrument, I could see the shine from the metal glimmer as The Cat brought it lower and lower. Fear was rising as a throat full of bile, too quickly and with a sick taste. I begged The Cat once more not to go away because of my fear. I was going to see this out for as long as I could possibly sustain my awareness. Slowly, The

Cat placed the caliper onto my head, carefully, as though it was a medical instrument needing minute precision to handle.

My Dreaming awareness began to run out. The "realness" of The Cat began to slowly dissipate. Its weight lessened, the calipers disappeared, the air was clear of wild odor, and I was lying on my bed, my head turned to the left. Tracking the experience moment by moment as I lay perfectly still, suddenly the proverbial light bulb went on. The Cat was Power! Not before that moment had I put two and two together to make the connection! What have I done by offering worship to Power? Now that I was no longer Dreaming my embarrassment knew no limits! It was ludicrous to offer my devotion to a cat! To deities and divinity, maybe, but a cat! What was so urgently compelling that I would do such a thing?

Grabbing the telephone I dialed the number of a woman who had been teaching and guiding me. Blurting out my story, I tried not to sound as desperate as I felt. I tried to convey how seductive The Cat was, how each tantalizing second was an explosion of possibilities when in its presence. To have swooned with such a confession was as far from my experience as the core of the earth is from its surface, unfathomably far. This then is the danger of Power! The woman confirmed the nature of Power to entice beyond measure, to persuade beyond reason. Her last comment would take some unraveling. It was a rubric of Toltec wisdom. "That Power is the core of who we are, there is no distinction," she said.

Chapter 6 Workout:

1. Identify an event that now looking back, relates to the sorcery realm and you'd not seen it before. Trust that Power will bring one to mind as you place your attention on an event at this moment.

2. Recall a time when you surrendered your mind to your body. This can happen during bodywork, exercise, eating, and/or Dreaming. There is Power in allowing your body to function in the manner in which it is intended to function.

3. Have you "explained an experience" away? What happened? With your newfound knowledge on Power, could that experience now be viewed differently—from a perspective of Power?

4. Identify an energy enhancing action. Identify an energy depleting action. What action can you take to maximize an energy enhancing action today?

7.
The Hunt for Power

Familiar with thoughts inside my head that were not my own, I listened to them speak. "The eight sacred circles—it's time to go." I smiled at the memory of the dream several years previous in which I'd met a guide telling me to go to eight sacred circles. Upon questioning the guide as to where the circles were located, she looked at me sternly and disappeared. At the time I was disappointed at my own ineptness: how could I have asked such a stupid question? But now, hiking the cliff on my favorite side of the island, a long ago yet distinctly familiar voice, referred to them again. I let my mind stay at rest. What would come next? Immediately, I thought back to last weekend. On the opposite side of the island was a cave and in that cave I had encountered a lizard—although not any species of lizard known to be on the island—while Dreaming. I had awakened in the middle of the night to a very large lizard creeping slowly up my chest, right up to my lips. Purposefully, it placed its lips onto mine—a transmission—but of what?

It wasn't until the next morning as I groggily crawled out of the cave that my conscious awareness went into gear: "Ah, Power! It came as a lizard this time and not my beloved Cat!" The voice at the top of the cliff-side spoke again, clearly, distinctly, but without emotional attachment, "Go! Just as you did last weekend, find places where Power will manifest. Go hunt for eight sacred circles!"

"Hunting" is a term that is at the heart of what a warrior/sorcerer does. It is an act of such strategy and largesse that initially it sounds much like a devotee learning a martial art. The time, effort, and commitment it will take to turn someone into a "lean, mean, fighting machine" in any chosen martial art discipline is vast. In the case of martial arts, once the art is learned, that chosen discipline becomes an integral part of who that person is—in an instant, the art moves and breathes through the devotee, whether in defense, or in purposeful exhibition—and can become an immediate signal to what is happening in the moment. The same time, effort, and commitment from the warrior/sorcerer who hunts Power will net similar results. "Hunting" Power will put the warrior/sorcerer into the position of possessing a skill that will keep that warrior/sorcerer alive, for without the hunt there is no sustenance. Once the skill of hunting is developed the warrior/sorcerer will have the capability of going after anything, Power in this case, and tracking it down. The purpose for hunting Power is hopefully clear by now, but that leaves the nuts and bolts of how to go about the hunt unexplored. For the record: we hunt Power in order to engage with Power. And, in the end, our engagement with Power will determine the outcome of who we are as warrior/sorcerers. The hunt is that important!

What comes to mind when the word "hunt" is used in broad terms? Immediately upon hearing the word, acts of purpose and acts of death come to mind. The term conjures up acts of penetration, piercing, stabbing, tricking, and subterfuge. It speaks of patience, skill, life, death, and poignancy. If a hunt is completed, someone or something loses its life. The term is filled with pungency. There is a moment in which the hunt is consummated; the hunt becomes a complete act of dedication, of sacrifice. It can also evoke images of victory, ownership, and acquiescence. Surrender occurs; someone or something gives their all. Change occurs, all the way from a simple change in position to a profound metamorphosis in spirit. However, it is not the consummation in the act of hunting that is always the primary goal. Something else takes place in the hunting process, and that something else is what the warrior/sorcerer is grooming throughout the whole affair. The warrior/sorcerer is after the supreme act of paying attention. She is focused and aware of what is happening in the environment. In addition, she is focused on what is happening within herself. Every thought and feeling is attuned to the act of focusing our attention, a giving to that object in front of us which is our prey, whether that be an animal, a thought, a person, a mood, or our actions. Once the warrior/sorcerer grooms this attentive awareness she cannot fail in completing the task. The prey will become hers.

The hunter, or warrior/sorcerer, equips herself for the hunt by attending to several things: the lay of the land, tools of the hunt, and timing. It requires knowledge of all three to make the hunt successful. The "lay of the land" can represent anything including actual landmass, moods and patterns of thought, relational exchanges whether internal or external, perceptions and states of awareness, objects, time or space. It is literally anything that has the potential of impacting the well being of the warrior/sorcerer. Important to dispel is the notion that whatever the hunter is hunting is an enemy. It is not always the case that the prey is an enemy. What we hunt can be as annoying as a mosquito buzzing on a sweltering day, an annoyance but not a deadly enemy. On the opposite extreme, the prey can be as significant as life and death; either the hunter or the hunted is going to go down in the end. Power in this context is an enemy until the warrior/sorcerer can command it, then it becomes the warrior/sorcerer's trusted confidante. This will occur differently for every warrior/sorcerer. It is the moment when Power ceases to be an enemy and becomes instead a rightful inheritance.

The "lay of the land" must be studied because we do not want it to become the weak point during the hunt. I learned this during one of my first hunts for Power to my eight sacred circles. When first staying overnight in the cave, I prepared for the overnight venture by carrying copious items of camping gear just in case I might need, say, an air mattress to go underneath the sleeping bag to ease my sleep. I didn't want to wile the night away tossing and turning on a bed of hard packed dirt and risk not going into a Dreaming state while sleeping—my focus would have become scattered and lacking the cohesion necessary for Dreaming. Or, a more abstract example: when I first began to hunt specific moods that held me captive by their nature of being habitual, I would readily explain their existence from a psychological point of view. But doing so would only give me a sense of liberty to "understand" them rather than to eradicate them. This was tantamount to mowing weeds at the same time as one mows the grass, leaving the roots from the weeds intact only to emerge again with new growth. Recognizing the "lay of the land" assisted me in knowing that the mood itself didn't merely need to be curbed, but that the mood needed to be released entirely from my fund of emotional responses.

The lay of the land can also help determine the tools necessary for the hunt. Useless to use an Uzi to kill a gnat or try to take down an elephant with a pellet gun! The hunter learns to match the weapon used with the prey she seeks. In addition, the warrior/sorcerer will be better at using certain weapons as opposed to using others. Sometimes the things we most want to get rid of or to let go of can become resistant to the tool used against them. In effect, their tolerance level for eradication rises.

I was married for many years. For a portion of that time, about a third of the way into the length of the marriage, we went to a therapist for couple's counseling. What we were doing was hunting down those internal and external communication issues that were negatively affecting our relationship. The counseling was a godsend; both of us came to a better awareness of those behaviors that continued to snag us, and that drained the goodness from the relationship. Going to see a therapist fed our relationship in a healthy way.

Eventually, however, I left the marriage because hunting relational issues between us didn't sustain the marriage for me over time. No amount of therapy was going to ignite a flame of love for my husband, nor ratify my feelings about continuing the marriage. My tolerance level for understanding, accepting, or working on the relationship was not going to increase. More therapy wasn't going to change my feelings for him and hold together a relationship that was over. But I didn't recognize this initially and continued to use the same tool by focusing it in another direction. More about this in a moment.

The prey that is particularly elusive may need to be hunted with various weapons at any given time. Sometimes, it may be easier to take down a wild hare with a bow and arrow than with a rifle. Switching to an example in the field of my education, psychology is an excellent tool for Tracking down repetitive behavioral patterns, habitual thoughts and emotions, and systems dynamics. Psychology can answer for any and all of those behaviors and emotions should they be considered something to be changed. As a field of beliefs about the mind however, psychology can become a trap unto itself; it can hinder the warrior/sorcerer from launching beyond its boundaries, as we've already noted earlier.

Take the example of my marriage. After ending couple's therapy, I entered an analysis. For those unfamiliar with this form of therapy, it is when a client sees a psychoanalyst, "lying on the couch" for three or four times a week for a number of years. It is extensive and exhaustive attention paid to the individual self as they encounter their environment and those in it. Since the couple's therapy had come to an end, I chose another "weapon" to hunt down my relationship disturbances. This tool, while useful for a time, again was outgrown. Psychology had become an overused tool, ineffective to resolve what I was after. My dilemma can also be described with the analogy of trying to build a house with a hammer—there are some aspects of construction that are going to take more than a hand tool used for pounding!

The last aspect of hunting that needs to be identified before the actual hunt begins is timing. Timing is everything for a successful hunt! A hunter going to the water hole midday on the Savanna isn't likely to find much game lurking around despite knowing how to locate the watering spot and carrying his best weapon. I would even push this to an extreme statement: timing is of the Other! Warrior/sorcerers need to tap into timing as a synergistic quality that brings everything together. Before you think, "What are you talking about?" let me explain, first with an example and then with the principle I am suggesting.

Remember when I mentioned earlier that for a period of a year or so I made every attempt, apart from going to the dark alley on the wrong side of the tracks, to get hallucinogens? I asked people, I looked for openings at work, I wrote acquaintances from the past, I approached sympathetic friends, and no way, no how could I hunt down the Power plants I wanted. And then magically they appeared. They became available for my exploration. At the time, I didn't really grasp the principle of timing. I attributed the experience to one of inadequacy on my part rather than that the timing was off, or that there was anything to this quality of "timing." Timing is of the Other. Power is available all the time, anyplace, anywhere—but until the warrior/sorcerer is ready to engage with it she doesn't take notice or will attribute the lack to her own folly. Until the warrior/sorcerer recognizes Power and calls it to her it is nowhere; it cannot be found.

The warrior/sorcerer is ready; she has an awareness of the environment, she brings with her the tools with which to hunt, and she grasps that timing is critical to her success. She enters the situation—the lay of the land—and positions herself. There are three more aspects to hunting Power that she now attunes to. The first is to be still. The prey is not likely to walk into her hands and is far more likely to be aware of the hunter long before the hunter is aware of the prey. When hunting animals it is easy to speak in these terms; the animals are sensing and conscious beings who can determine sooner than we when something is odd or out of place or foreign to their natural abode. But what if the warrior/sorcerer is hunting down a recurring pattern of thought? What if the warrior/sorcerer is hunting Power within her Dreaming? Are these conscious aspects that sense our approach? The activity of being still will help to determine the enemy we are approaching—Power is certainly aware of when the warrior/sorcerer seeks to engage with it. Being still will allow the hunter to seek the object being hunted without initial interference—it is the act that puts the warrior/sorcerer into position to consummate the act of hunting. If the warrior/sorcerer cannot be still and quiet, she runs the risk of never eyeing the prey at all and thereby losing by default.

The act of being still is a hunter's strategy. Being still may require extended amounts of involvement with time and this is where the concept intercepts with timing; the two go hand in hand. Once I become still on a hunt, I can best determine when to strike. For example, say I am in a meditative state in order to gain gnosis on a subject. I am still and quiet;

Encounter with Power

my thoughts are minimal, if not absent entirely. Because I am still, my internal screen or the blackness in front of my closed eyelids is blank. There is no thought, yet I know I am seeking something, something that will inform me about my query. I am seeking Power in the form of knowledge. Suddenly, an image flies by—it almost runs off the edge of the blackness before I grab it. But I lunge at it like a frog's tongue jets out to grasp the insect. That image caught in stillness will inform me, it will give the knowledge that I seek.

Just before lying down in a circle with the group for a group meditation, I arose to go to the bathroom. The ending meditation was my favorite part of the evening; it always held mystery and the opportunity for exploration. I headed for the bathroom with the upcoming meditation present on my mind. Seating myself on the toilet, I glanced up as my eye caught a sudden movement. Fluttering along the top of the ceiling was the largest moth I had ever seen! It was a dusky, charcoal gray moth with a wingspan of nearly four inches. In an erratic flight pattern it appeared to swerve, dip, and roll without direction. It was not in its natural habitat, and it knew it. For me, it was an omen loud and clear. What was the moth announcing? I Tracked what my thoughts had been just prior to seeing it. Ah, the meditation. I would pay close attention to what happened during the meditation.

Instantly, as the meditation got under way, I could feel my body relax into the rhythm of the bowl. The woman facilitating the meditation for the group played a large, crystal bowl that would always send my spirit flying. Sound immediately put me into a deep meditative state. Tonight was no different. My mind was still and I was in the black void. Without warning, the lavender crystal was visible in the black void all around me. A large lavender crystal was positioned in the corner of the room as were various other stones, shells, rattles, and drums. This was the first time one of the objects had addressed me directly. "Is there a message for me?" I asked, aware that I could also be in the presence of that crystal without any intended message due to its sheer loveliness.

"Don't abandon your self to anything," the crystal stated clearly, and then it was gone! The rest of the meditation I rolled that thought around and around in my head, dipping and turning it over within. Just like the moth flying in the bathroom clearly out of its familiar element, this koan would swirl and dive and flutter due to its unfamiliar presence in my mind. Until its relevance became clear, I would continue to hunt what its appearance meant for me, and how it had the potential to impact my life. In fact, waiting for the meaning of knowledge to unfold moves the warrior/sorcerer into the next strategy of the hunt.

The next strategy used by the warrior/sorcerer is to wait. Waiting is a lifelong task for the warrior/sorcerer. But rather than to feel as though the waiting is laborious, the warrior/sorcerer knows that all is in place; she has positioned herself with the tools she needs and that is all she need do. The act of hunting does not guarantee a return of prey. The warrior/sorcerer knows that even though she may not gain prey in the hunt she has gained from being still and waiting. There are experiences to be gained in those endeavors alone! Waiting teaches patience and forbearance; there is nothing to be had in a hurry—hurry eats up personal power. Waiting gives us the liberty to be free from doing anything, precisely because we are prepared and have taken the necessary steps in order to be waiting in the first place. Waiting is not stalling or the state of doing nothing without former preparation. The warrior/sorcerer is not in repose without a weapon or tool—she is waiting with full alertness, eyes wide open. At any moment she is prepared for action. Waiting is not sedentary; it is fully engaged in the moment at hand.

And so the prey appears. It may look like we expected; it may look nothing like what we expected. The surprise component of the hunt is palpable. What if the hunter has set a trap for a brown bear and a grey wolf steps into it instead? What if the warrior/sorcerer hunts Power and it is not at all what she envisioned it to be? She has studied her enemy, she knows the locale, her timing is right on, and Power steps forward. Power ends up being a Cat that comes to you while Dreaming, placing its heavy body on top of your head positioned on the pillow, lowering itself until you cannot suck air in to breathe. Or, Power enables you to end a friendship that no longer serves your intended goal of freedom. Or, Power comes as an ongoing confidence and assuredness that your plan of action is on target. Although the prey may be a surprise, it can also be exactly what you set out to accomplish—either way, the hunt is completed—an act has been performed that builds on your ability and skill as a warrior/sorcerer.

Waiting for the unfolding of the message from the gray moth took six months' time. Throughout that period, I Tracked what I historically abandoned myself to: ideologies and systems of knowledge. Remember, I loved to figure things out and to put things together like a puzzle! I had followed the system of religion and the paradigm of psychoanalysis for many, many years. What was the harm in abandoning myself to those or other pursuits? Turns out, I very nearly abandoned myself again to a set of ideologies that were not my own. Hunting down this tendency to want others to tell me how to direct my life, to be willing to abandon myself to someone in order for them to tell me how to live as a warrior/sorcerer was exactly what the moth and the crystal were warning me about. Hadn't I learned from my experience of devoting myself to Carlos Castaneda and all that he wrote instead of surrendering to the knowledge he shared? This would be a prey that had earth-shattering consequences! I would end up leaving friendships, putting closure to relationships, and striking out on my own as a warrior/sorcerer—all because I hunted down a point of view that I had abandoned myself to without an awareness of its full impact on my evolution.

One last aspect of hunting needs exploration before we talk about changing our terms. The phrase, although differently worded for every culture, carries the same spirit behind it: take only what is needed. The warrior/sorcerer doesn't hunt in excess; she doesn't take a caribou, a wolf, and a fox when she only needs dinner for the night. In writing this portion, I wanted a visceral example. I understood the concept behind not being greedy or taking in excess, but I wanted an example that felt vital and alive to this very evening of writing on this chapter.

Lying in bed before dropping off to sleep I focused with my entire awareness on Dreaming about whether or not a warrior/sorcerer could actually take too much Power. We have the Universe for our playground; why would we limit ourselves? Why not hunt as much as is possible?

Throughout the evening, I would have a dream, awaken, write it down, go back to sleep, enter Dreaming, awaken, write some more, fall back into sleep, dream, awaken—and so the evening went. Some of the dreams held symbolism, some of them were Dreaming, one dream was a nightmare, one Dream was spoken words—all of them a feast from altered realities. Never before had I dreamed with as much profusion and loquacity. As I crawled out of bed the next morning the understanding hit me square between the eyes: the Dreams were an implosion of Power; I had dined and overstuffed! Yes, Power can be hunted in excess! Yes, too much Power is a waste of Spirit. Yes, Power is useless if used wantonly. Hunt Power as needed and leave the rest for the next time a hunt is on.

The hike to Mouna Kea—the volcano on the Big Island that is home to thirteen observatories from around the world—was a hunt for Power. In a rented car (don't tell Alamo!), we drove just below 13,000 feet in order to hike forty-five minutes to one of the highest lakes in the world. The lake is stunning: a relatively small reservoir that is internally fed with underground melt year around. With no greenery to speak of except for the algae that glows an eerie green on the edges of the ice-cold water, the lake ripples with a mystical wind. The wind blows across the iron red and ashen gray volcanic rock, circumscribing it in every direction, hitting the lake like hundreds of soft reverberations of unspoken sound.

It is my second pilgrimage to the lake and, odd as it may sound, it is the path to the lake that captures my soul. Panting and moving slowly due to lack of oxygen (or, the presence of Power), I place one foot after the other in front of me. My friends are behind for I want to commune with the path alone. Last time I was here, the rocks cried out, calling, cajoling, inviting, entreating me to pay attention—and I did. Here I am again. I open myself to what is available: anything and everything that I might connect with here on this faintly worn path that clears my thoughts and moves my spirit. I pause to breathe evenly; I know others who experience headaches, stomach pain, disorientation, and nausea as they walk the same path. I turn to see my friends walking, walking slowly and laboriously behind me a hundred yards. Again, the path speaks to me of what has been troubling me. There is no glossing of words, no fancy elocution, and no unnecessary verbiage. I wait.

"You must let her go. Her friendship with you is causing you imbalance. Look! She is far behind you on the trail. Do you see that she needs assistance? It is not your assistance that she needs. In order for you to move forward, you must let her drop behind." The message is clear. It is not muddled with my emotions, excuses, and empathy. Those things have kept me linked to her. "After all," I had told myself, "friends stick by one another, don't they?" The crisp, cool air has cleared my thinking and my heart is pounding without falter. All of my defenses fall to the ground.

Another friend approaches and smiles. I look at her with sudden tears filling my eyes. "It's happening again," I say as though that explains everything. "This is a holy mountain," I whisper reverently.

She returns the reverence with a smile of her own. "It spoke to me, too." This is her first trip to the lake but there is no need to say more or to explain. I want to stay forever. I remember other experiences that move my very being to such a sublime place. The disciples of Jesus felt this same way while on a hike with him to a mountaintop. They implored him to allow them to build a temple on the holy spot and remain time immemorial. I, too, would stay forever if I could, for I cannot always hear so clearly amidst my fellow beings at lower altitudes. Air enters my lungs and I breathe it in evenly. I am breathing in the Spirit of this holy place.

Chapter 7 Workout:

1. Set up a hunt for Power either through identifying self-importance that needs let go of or working with omens. This will require that you be able to track your own actions carefully in order to catch the nuances of behavior you perform routinely rather than purposefully.

2. Hunting is about paying attention. What can you pay attention to in your thoughts that can become a hunt for Power?

3. Are there tools that you have overused in hunting, tools that need to be abandoned for newer ones?

4. Recognize the strategies for the hunt: "lay of the land", tools for the hunt, and timing. Identify each of these strategies within an experience you have had.

5. How does timing impact a hunt?

6. Have you hunt to excess? What were the results?

8.

The Power in Dreaming

    The Shaman speaks softly to the circle of women, asking four dreamers to bring their Dreaming back to the group on the morrow. I raise my hand, offering to Dream from the South direction. Nervous at my boldness in offering to Dream for the group I return quickly to the cabin and prepare to go to sleep. What if I don't go into Dreaming? What if I have nothing to report to the twenty women tomorrow morning, seated around the large stone bear placed in the center of the meeting hall? What will I say?

    The night is long. I toss and turn. I am waiting too eagerly, wanting too compulsively to go into the Dreaming state that usually is easy to access. Yet, I know I can Dream. All my life I've been a friend with my dreams, going to them when troubled or lonely or questioning. But I've never demanded a Dream. I've never required that I perform in a public forum the ability that comes easily while at home. It is early morning. With my eyes clamped shut I roll over and face the wall, positioning the blankets to cover my shoulders in the crisp, cold air from the Montana morning. The stillness is deafening. Suddenly, I dream of Red; there are three images that appear before me. I wait for more but the internal screen goes black. I grab the images. If I don't hold onto them they will disappear as I awaken.

    "Who is our dreamer to bring us a Dream from the South?" asks the Shaman. I raise my hand. Since breakfast I have been pondering the images. They are mysterious and not yet decoded. "I dreamt of three images. The first was a bear with the marks of her own kind raking down her chest, dripping

with blood. The second was of bear scat—it is fresh on the ground mingled with blood red berries. The third is a gently moving river, wide and deep and flowing blood red."

Five years later, I am hiking early in the morning. It is the time when the trail speaks clearly. "Remember the Dream in Montana? It is time for a new rendering of the three images." I wait breathlessly. I have worked extensively with the meaning of the first two images, but the third image has always been shrouded and obscure as though its significance has been kept from me. "The images speak of initiation, letting go, and passionate movement. Or, you can look at them as past, present, and future. You have completed the past and the present. Move into the future, the red river providing sustenance, Power, and movement. It has become your Now, it is who you are."

Dreaming is awareness. It is tempting to assume that "awareness" means the same thing as "to be aware" but that assumption is not accurate. We will take a look at the statement as it relates to the warrior/sorcerer pulling one more arrow out of her sling in an attempt to encounter Power. Dreaming comes in any number of forms although the act itself is always about shifting our perceptual abilities. The specific use by the warrior/sorcerer involves the use of her awareness; therefore we'll take a look at that concept in greater detail than previously. We will then move into a discussion of the many faces of Dreaming and how any number of them can be utilized by the warrior/sorcerer to access Power. We'll highlight a number of those forms, as each and every warrior/sorcerer will utilize them differently and with varying emphasis.

We'll then explore how Dreaming can be dangerous. This can only be a well-known statement by now: dealing with Power is dangerous. How does the warrior/sorcerer approach the state of Dreaming knowing that it can be dangerous? Dreaming initially occurs outside of our normal awareness but its vast potential for building and sustaining our contact with Power is legion in the Toltec realm. We want to be able to develop our Dreaming to the point that we are conscious and volitional while in a state that is usually either romanticized or marginalized. Doing so will build our awareness, a state of being that naturally increases our Power. We approach the state of Dreaming with openness and without fear. We know that our available Power will call to us the level of Dreaming that we have the capacity to interact with at any given moment.

The most potent route to Dreaming, without the use of hallucinogens, is through nighttime dreams. The distinction between Dreaming and dreaming is a good place to begin. The two are initially experienced as the same thing but this is due to a lack of differentiation or experience on the part of the warrior/sorcerer. Dreaming with a lower case "d" is what occurs nightly during REM sleep. Dreaming with an upper case "D" is the location of alternative worlds to be explored by the warrior/sorcerer due to the placement of her awareness. Even though the visual content of the dream can be the same while Dreaming or in dreaming, the experience for the warrior/sorcerer will be entirely different. Due to the body's natural tendency to shift perception while sleeping, the warrior/sorcerer has ready access to this state. Our mind is at rest (at least relatively speaking) while asleep and this allows us to experience altered perception without the bias that is present while not sleeping. The warrior/sorcerer aims to take advantage of this unique vantage point while sleeping.

This concept of awareness has already been mentioned in passing. Remember the story of the evening hike to the cliff side when a loud laugh announced someone was present along with my friend and I as we hiked along? I was aware that the laugh was Power whereas my friend believed the laugh came from a woman seated behind us on the wall alongside the path. Awareness is the location that our energy body places focus on at any given moment. It is an act of the body, not of the mind. "To be aware" is a function of the mind, whereas "awareness" is a perceptual act of the body. It takes practice to shift from one to the other. The warrior/sorcerer wants to cultivate awareness because it aids in Dreaming. Awareness allows the warrior/sorcerer access to being lucid while Dreaming that allows for contact with Power. As we build our awareness we are also building our capacity to engage with and to increase our contact with Power.

I am ten years old and in love with my dreams. Every night I eagerly wait going to sleep because I know what will happen. It is as predictable as getting up the next morning and eating a bowl of cereal. In fact, some nights I can make the same dream happen, although I'm not quite sure how I do it. It seems as though if I long for the dream with all of my being it comes to me. It is the dream in which I can fly.

Barely rising above the telephone poles and rooftops that I can clearly view under me, I practice lifting myself higher and higher. Navigating carefully, I am more and more aware that the position of my arms and how I position my legs makes a difference in how high I can rise in the air. Every night I concentrate on adjusting my body so the flight will be smooth and exhilarating. The feeling of freedom in moving through the air without wings never leaves me. I long for the feeling every night of my ten year old life.

Odd as it may sound there is a feeling that comes from my body that determines whether or not my flight will be successful or not. When it is present, the flight will be without mishap. When it is not present, I will struggle to fly high enough to clear the electrical lines and rooftops. I am a warrior/sorcerer in training, but I'm not yet aware of it on a conscious level. What I am clearly in touch with is the feeling of awareness—when I have that indescribable feeling of knowing something without knowing it in my mind, I move with a sense of purpose, surrendering to the feeling that will then guide me. Without it, I am simply a ten-year-old girl, engaging in flights of sexual fantasy, as any psychologist might interpret the dream.

Nighttime dreams offer the easiest route to Dreaming proper but there are other means of going into Dreaming. Other forms of Dreaming include meditation, early morning gnosis, Dreaming awake and journeying. A warrior/sorcerer will oftentimes find a particular bent for one method over another, or one method will suit you well during a phase of growth and then will drop by the wayside as you develop and mature. The warrior/sorcerer has freedom to pursue any or all; watch for any techniques described in the following that sound appealing and pursue it until you reach the state of Dreaming.

Meditation gives the mind freedom from the mediocrity of mentality. To allow our minds to stop chattering is an accomplishment sought by many who recognize that the mind can be at rest. The mind does not have to continually provide us with feedback, advice, information, emotions, and beliefs, in other words, non-stop talk. What happens when the mind stops all of this busyness? The mind does what it is designed to do: provide the cognition necessary to function in the daily world of humanity. It isn't a full time occupation although it seems to be from observing the masses. For a warrior/sorcerer who stops all of the internal chatter, she is able to access a meditative state and from there go into Dreaming. In other words, meditation offers the platform from which to dive into the practice of Dreaming.

Early morning meditation works well for me. In the early morning everyone in the house is still asleep—their energy is quiet, and this stillness allows easier movement into a meditative state. My mind is silent; its screen is blank. I experience nothing, or expressed another way, "no thing." The sublime feeling of "no thing" is a catapult for me into Dreaming. The Dreaming state puts me into a state of being that easily accesses knowledge. This knowledge is from the deep, dark recesses of all that a warrior/sorcerer has access to when placing her awareness onto "no thing." It is the place of Power. If I desire this knowledge, it doesn't show; when I have no expectations, it shows itself easily. This morning is no exception. Suddenly, I fully grasp the knowledge that my feeling state is in my body, primarily in my muscles and body organs. At the age of seven or eight that feeling state shifted from my limbs, organs, skin, and flesh "up" into my mind and it has reigned there ever since. (Hence, my struggles to fly while Dreaming when ten years old.) My work as a masseuse has been geared toward getting that feeling state back to its rightful home, outside of the thought process that is my mind, and back into my body. At the moment, my physical body is total stillness. It feels as though it's in a state of paralysis—a heaviness which is a signpost for me that I am Dreaming. I take this knowledge back with me into an awakened state. It will be the catalyst for change on many levels.

Early morning gnosis has a rather unpleasant sounding title: hypnagogic state. It is a state in which the mind is neither asleep nor awake; it is in a lull. That peculiar lull in consciousness can be focused on and Tracked for Dreaming purposes. What is critical to attend to in this state is where the warrior/sorcerer's attention is focused. It is often the case that you can awaken out of sleep, lie peacefully, and be without thought. You are in the hypnagogic state. Follow where or what your awareness brings before you. Because the Dreaming state is outside of the conscious control of the mind, the warrior/sorcerer's thought process is not the same as when awake. It is not simply a matter of thinking in an accustomed manner. What bubbles up is a connection to the Other; it is a link with knowledge and Power that is not as easily accessed when the mind is fully operational.

Once recognized and given permission to operate, that lull will teach the warrior/sorcerer those mysteries that are harder come by when fully awake. With practice, the warrior/sorcerer can access this peculiar state with ease and will easily recognize when the mind comes into play. The distinction between the two is apparent with practice. In effect, this state clears the channels for incoming knowledge uninterrupted by the thought process. Whatever comes feels as though it is heightened in intensity; the knowledge is astoundingly clear and without prejudice from the mind. When the mind intercedes, the resultant thoughts are heavy and dense. The feeling is one of a great distance being traveled at extreme speeds between the two states. It's like traveling in an elevator the distance of a hundred floors in the space of a few seconds.

I was not asleep, nor was I awake. A voice sounded, "Her passion needs to be destroyed." Instantly, I felt fear. What passion? Who was the voice referring to? Quickly, I got out of bed to write the statement down. Too often I had told myself, "I'll remember," but I would experience amnesia within moments of rousing out of bed. I knew that early morning gnosis often spoke to me in koans, but I had no clear idea what this one meant. This is a good place to announce that Dreaming doesn't always make sense. It isn't always easily understood by our rational minds. Dreaming is an affront to our minds! The content of our Dreaming easily becomes a maze of misunderstood meaning to our mind. In this instance my mind balked at the sentence, "Her passion needs to be destroyed." In the end however, the koan led me into shifting my perception of "who I thought

I was as a writer" to "who I am as a writer." The two were stuck together as a belief for too, too long, and unbeknownst to me, they needed to be dynamited apart. Suffice it to say, this early morning gnosis exploded the placement of my awareness from one perception to another—and I was clueless that either one had existed in the first place! Power will confront our self-importance if we're open to being taught through our Dreaming!

Dreaming awake is another form of Dreaming to access Power. As I write about these different states of Dreaming I am acutely aware that the labels for the different experiences are arbitrary and assigned. More precisely, the experiences are not different but the means of access to the experiences are different. As the warrior/sorcerer experiences the various means of experiencing an altered perception on her own feel free to assign definitions to them that fit for you. There is no proper label. I have heard various warrior/sorcerers assign names to the states different than my own, but in discussion we discover that our experiences are similar in nature. The most important thing for the warrior/sorcerer to do is to put her self in the position to have her own experience. I cannot emphasize this often enough. Identification, clarification, and categorizing can become a stumbling block if insisted upon too early; performing these mental activities takes away from having the experience itself.

What is Dreaming awake? Dreaming awake happens when your eyes are open. Dreaming awake can occur anywhere, while standing in a line at the grocery store, while driving in a car, while seated at a park, while lying down. It is a natural shift of our perceptive abilities (as are all of the Dreaming techniques.) While hiking in the hills of Southern California one hot summer day, I glanced up to see a red tailed hawk flying high above me. He looked postage stamp size but I could make out his familiar rusty red tail feathers. I gazed uninterruptedly as he swooped and glided on the unseen air currents. In an instant, I was catapulted up into the air. Now I was the one who was flying gracefully in the blue stillness looking down at a two-legged standing on the dry river rocks looking up into the sky. An instant later, and I was standing again in the canyon streambed.

A second example occurred while I was hiking in the jungle green that ceaselessly covers the island of Hawaii. As I placed my feet between the exposed roots from tall, thin eucalyptus roots covering the trail, my mind was in a quiet state. Suddenly, out of my left peripheral vision, I caught sight of a large black panther traveling quietly beside me. My companion was silent witness to the Power of that place. The veil between the daily dream we live and the Other positioned around the warrior/sorcerer at all times is thin and permeable when Dreaming awake.

Journeying is a broad category but easily practiced and developed. It has been termed guided imagery and/or shamanic journeying. It is accessed through listening to sound that is specifically designed to put the body into a meditative state, whether that is the sound of drum beats, or multi-layered sound that accesses the brain's capacity to equalize two different beats. Journeying can occur while dancing, in a sweat lodge, while walking, while lying in bed. Using drumming, listening to a CD, or being seated inside a lodge filled with extreme heat, can assist the warrior/sorcerer to engage easily. Common for the warrior/sorcerer when beginning to travel realms other than the consensus reality she may be most familiar with is to hear voices calling, sounds such as pops, squeaks, and cracks, telephones ringing, and doors knocking. These sounds are calls from Spirit. The warrior/sorcerer is being summoned and invited to a Dreaming reality apart from daily life.

The silver black wings spread once more across my line of vision. I am in a coniferous forest and the sight of a crow flying through the pine bearing branches of the trees is odd. I am accustomed to seeing crows flying over the high desert shrubs of the local canyons. For the third time, a crow flies in front of me. Three times the same animal appears in my line of vision. At that moment, I hear the drum begin to beat evenly and slowly signaling for return. As an even rhythm is sounded, I bring myself back into the room. The forest recedes and the crow disappears. I lay in a circle on the carpet with a dozen people all returning from their own journeys of discovery.

Steven, the workshop leader, had directed the participants to go into a meditative state with the beat of the drum. After traveling through a

Encounter with Power

tunnel we were to invite an animal spirit to come to us. "Watch carefully. The power animal will cross your path three times. This will be the signal for that animal to interact with you," Steven had instructed.

For the next five years, Crow would continue to fly to me, to speak with me, and to guide me—all manifestations of Power to teach me on this Toltec path. This method of Dreaming is easily practiced and is a profound means of providing instruction, healing, knowledge, and guidance. Without even being aware of it, the warrior/sorcerer is practicing her awareness and allowing that awareness to inform her of the creativity that Power brings; she is literally Dreaming through the innate power of sound.

Initially, there is a common tendency for the warrior/sorcerer to treat Dreaming as though it is tangential to daily living, or at worst, illusory. This is a grave mistake! Dreaming is a state of such accessibility to Power that the warrior/sorcerer doesn't want to squander it. To do so would be a waste of Power. What can easily happen is that the warrior/sorcerer is either unaware of the Power in Dreaming, or is unable to experience it for herself. There is a means of challenging this stalemate though, and the means of challenge for the warrior/sorcerer is simple. The same thing I did as a ten year old before going to bed each evening can be the same thing that the warrior/sorcerer can also do for her self. Long to go into Dreaming. Look forward with every fiber of your being to accessing that state. Practice the other means of encountering Power such as lessening self importance, sustaining those experiences with Power that you do have, Track throughout the day, and hunt Power whenever and wherever you can. Dreaming will happen. Because it is the realm of Power, Dreaming will happen for the warrior/sorcerer who readies her self for the battle. It is simply a matter of preparedness and timing for the warrior/sorcerer with awareness.

There is danger in Dreaming that needs to be addressed before we end this chapter. The danger comes in extremes for the warrior/sorcerer who allows the Power in Dreaming to overcome them. The danger in one extreme has already been addressed: beware of treating Dreaming as though it is not real, as though it has no impact on you whatsoever! This is a mindset that is dangerous because it can cause you to go headlong into Dreaming that you may not be prepared for. Going into Dreaming is like going to a foreign country and being vulnerable to differences in weather, culture, food, communication, and language. When we travel to a completely foreign country we are going to be out of our element with regards to all of these variables unless we go prepared. No one can survive going to the Himalayas in wintertime wearing a pair of shorts. They won't stay alive for very long! Believe it or not, warrior/sorcerers can make decisions while Dreaming that are not in their best interest, decisions that can cause their energy bodies harm. Treating Dreaming as though it is not "real" can be deadly! A warrior/sorcerer can lose her battle with Power while Dreaming!

The opposite end of the spectrum involves succumbing to the allure and seductiveness that Dreaming offers. Lucid dreaming is a good example. Lucid dreaming is commonly known as the knowledge that one is dreaming while in the dream state. It is not only desirable for the warrior/sorcerer, but it is also the gateway into Dreaming proper. The awareness that one is lucid while Dreaming allows the warrior/sorcerer to take action; and that is the sine qua non of Toltec behavior—to act, even in Dreaming. A more accurate statement would be to say that action is called for particularly while Dreaming. This is due to being in a state of unequaled Power since Dreaming is the fountainhead of Power itself. But the allure of being lucid while Dreaming can cause the warrior/sorcerer to become fixated on trivialities and to take no action whatsoever.

Wandering through a large home, I am transfixed by the items I see all around me. I know that I am leaving the home for good, but it falls to me to look over all of the things in the home to evaluate whether or not to keep them or to junk them. Hundreds and hundreds of items have been collected—someone was certainly diligent in gathering so many things! The trinkets, craft items, and art pieces are beautiful. I walk slowly through the house. Every piece is fascinating to stare at! There are pieces of blown glass, Lladro figurines, Limoges vases, cups and saucers, Fiesta ware, and bronze pieces. The variety and numbers are more than I can possibly count. I walk along looking lovingly at items that I recognize. It has taken years to collect all of these! Now I am responsible to determine whether they stay or whether they go.

The color and depth of everything has captured me. I stare at one blown glass vase, looking intently at the lines of rainbow color—how did the artist include all of the colors in such a tiny, five inch vase? I stare with a feeling of total fascination. The depth of the color is rich and deep giving me the feeling that the colors are alive. I recognize that I am Dreaming. The colors are more vibrant than "real" life; they have intensity to them that I never recognize while awake. I love this feeling of jubilance while Dreaming! It is as though everything I encounter feels pure and undiluted by the concerns of daily life. I continue to look at the vase. It has captured every particle of my awareness! I remind myself to look away. "Don't stare! Move your eyes around the room, see what else is here for you to take in."

Looking down at my hands I see a pink, fur lined handbag. My wallet is missing. I will need my wallet sooner or later; it contains my credit cards and cash. Panic causes me to feel helpless. What will I do? Without thought, I make the decision to stop the panic. Instantly, the panic disappears. I walk outside. Spontaneously, I hold the handbag up to the house that holds those hundreds of trinkets inside. The house has large, grey eyes. Shouting forcefully, I demand, "Give it back! Put it back in my purse. Now!" No conscious thought identifies the house as the culprit, but I know without thought that the house had stolen my power to take care of myself and all of those trinkets were part of the subterfuge. I look down at the pink handbag. The wallet is back inside.

Shifting out of Dreaming, I lie in bed. My body feels as though a mild electrical current is running through it—without harm to me, but instead providing a sense of well being that I thrive on for the remaining two hours before dawn. I go over and over the Dreaming in my mind trying to recapture the feeling of wonder and awe inside of the house, of command at confronting the grey eyes and receiving back the contents of my wallet, of the electrical current continuing to enliven my body. I recognize that I was almost trapped by that vase! How preposterous! At the same time, I exult in having left the house and having received my wallet back from those large, doe eyes. I had acted volitionally, escaping the tendency to get caught up in the detail of the Dreaming, thereby squandering my available Power.

You may notice that there has been no discussion on the meaning and interpretation of dreams. This was intentional. It is not to imply that working with the symbols and meaning of dreams is not a worthy endeavor, because it can be. I have worked with dreams for many years and have learned a wealth of knowledge about my self and others in this way. Dreams can be accessed for divination, medical and spiritual healing, foretelling, visions, and psychological uncovering and processing. Since the purpose of this chapter was to look at Dreams through the lens of Power, I chose to set aside that treasure chest that dreaming can be. Instead, I concentrated on what Dreaming can do for the warrior/sorcerer pursuing an encounter with Power. Power shapes the warrior/sorcerer's Dreaming as much as the warrior/sorcerer shapes Power through her Dreaming—the two form an inseparable pair awesome to behold!

After I undress and am lying on the massage table, Bruce enters the little room that is as warm as an oven in a bakery.

"How are you?" he asks.

"I'm worried. My back is sore from moving a huge shelf unit in the garage and now there's a lump midway down my back. I think I'd better go see a chiropractor—I know that type of injury isn't your focus—but maybe you could look at it."

Bruce looks carefully at where my hand is reaching over my shoulder to point out the sore spot. He nods assent as he runs his hand down my back stopping at the bulge on my right side.

"Let's see what we can do," he says as he turns to switch on some music. I smile at how he's included me in the task at hand. Even though I will lie on the massage table as he does the work I know that it is my willingness and openness to be there that will contribute to our success. The flute music instantly calms my worries as Bruce reaches for his bottle of oil and pours into his hand.

It takes only minutes for Bruce to concentrate with his hands on the swollen area. It takes even less time for his thumb and index finger to be placed together over the spot. A shiver of electricity begins to charge through my arms and converge into my scapula. Inhaling and exhaling forcefully, Bruce squeezes in a comment, "This may be painful—huh, huh, huh—there is a tremendous amount of energy here—haw, haw, haw—it seems to be caught between these two ribs." I lay quietly, erasing any thoughts from my mind. The flute continues its rhythmic pulse. The tingling of energy running though my arms diverts my attention from the pain as Bruce continues to hold his fingers still. Pressure increases on my back as though Bruce is taking his fingers and pushing forcefully. I know from past experience that this is not the case. Bruce maintains an equal amount of pressure with his fingers at any given moment. Odd, but soon I will forget that this is so. As Bruce follows the energy it begins to move. My shoulders, thighs, and buttocks tense with the perceived pressure. I moan intensely.

"I can't seem to maintain the right angle to keep in touch with this," Bruce says, perplexed. He repositions his fingertips. He gains contact again with the blocked energy. Slowly, and with a feeling of increasing agony, I feel his fingers begin to move around my side to just below my right breast. Suddenly, a sigh escapes him and he releases his fingers. I feel instantaneous relief at the same moment.

"There is a tremendous amount of energy here. I can feel my heart racing and the level of my own energy is extremely high," he comments as he returns to the same spot. His comments never have cause and effect attached to them. They are simple statements of awareness.

Images begin to flow through me. Bruce has taught me that they can be paired with the bodily experience; this is why there is an effort to clear the mind from the outset. These images are useful for diagnostic purposes both for the masseur and for the client. I begin to track them. With virile force, the image of the leathery breast from last week's dream appears.

"Oh my—!" I spit out as Bruce's hands push down. Again he follows the energy as he asks me to lift and slightly shift to my side as his hands return to my ribs under my right breast. The image I see is the brown breast from my dream squirting with watery milk full and warm and strengthening. The image dissipates as the pain at hand becomes paralyzing. An electric current is racing up and down my right arm. Bruce nearly turns me over as he holds

his fingers still and waits. Waiting with him, I breathe deeply as each gasp produces a sharp pain shooting up my arm. Bruce breathes haltingly—he too is caught in the intensity of the block.

"What's the image you have?"

"I can't—I've got to hold onto it." I squeeze my eyes shut as the image appears again. It is the large leathery breast with milk flowing freely. The pain is excruciating. I want to cry. The tears squeeze from the corners of my eyes. I can only concentrate on breathing; the tears will have to wait. I feel a release from the intense pain at nearly the same moment that Bruce releases his finger grip on me. Tears roll down my face.

Again, Bruce returns to the same point of contact.

"It's releasing but there is more," he explains. His fingers return to what is now home base for this session. He follows the moment of perceived energy with his fingers. As soon as he finds it, he quickly loses it. "Where did it go?" he seems bewildered. Contacting the energy apex he begins to follow it. Again, he loses it. I image the game of hide and seek.

"Where is it hiding?" I ask without feeling the need to define "it." Bruce will know what I am saying.

"I'm having a difficult time getting the right angle to keep in touch with it," he says. He works silently as I wait for him to accurately gain contact with the center of the painful spot. We are playing an exhaustive game of "catch as catch can" and we are coming up the losers.

"How can it hide from us?" I have personified "it" as an enemy that is fighting to keep from exposure. Silently I tell myself, "Let go." It is my belief that my mind needs to facilitate the movement in my body and to tell my body what to do. What I am profoundly experiencing is that the process is precisely the other way around. My body is directing the images in my mind in an effort to communicate. My mind is not the power fount I've always assumed it to be—the director running the show.

"Roll over and let's see what is happening on your front side," Bruce says. Slowly, because I am suddenly exhausted, I attempt to move. With a concentrated effort I try to move but my body stays mute. I feel disoriented as though my experience has erased my cognitive abilities. I'm not sure I know how to move.

"What do you want?" I ask to reassure myself that I have heard him. He repeats his request. "I want to cry," I sigh sorrowfully.

"Good, maybe that's what is needed," he answers gently.

"That felt like an evil spirit that wouldn't give up," I say with conviction as my body finally turns over and tears roll down my face once more. Surprised, Bruce looks at me with conviction that I can't interpret.

"Oh, really?" he asks rhetorically.

The breast image is back. Immediately, I want to ask Bruce about his finger grip on my breast. I want to tell him the image from the dream that held tenaciously onto me earlier, as he was pulling up on my breast with his fingers positioned on my nipple.

"I had a dream last weekend that I've returned to again and again this week," I say as I launch into the telling of my dream.

"The image was particularly strong when you were pulling my breast with your fingers. Remember, a few minutes ago, when I was on my side?" I question him to orient him to the moment I am referring to. He looks at me with wide eyes.

"I didn't have my fingers on your breast," he states clearly. Now my surprise is palpable.

"Yes, you were pulling up on my breast with your fingers and that's when the image of the breast from my dream was the strongest." Bruce holds up his hand, palm flat. "I had the palm of my hand flat on your breast like this," he motions with his head in the direction of his hand.

"Oh, my God! That's not what if felt like at all!" My mind cannot fathom what has happened.

"That is the image your mind gave to the experience," Bruce explains matter-of-factly. But the explanation sounds profound. The image of Bruce pulling something stubborn and resistant from out of me had been vivid. I had not even considered opening my eyes to verify how or where he was touching me. I trusted Bruce explicitly; he would never take advantage of me lying in such a vulnerable position on his massage table. In my mind Bruce had pulled something out of me with my breast as the contact point. And in my experience of lying on his massage table with my eyes tightly shut, my breast had merged

130

with the leathery brown breast from my dream a week ago. My mind had an agenda my Dreaming had not indicated to be the case at all.

Bruce began to work up and down with his hands gliding smoothly the length of my body. Soon he held his hands about eight inches off the table. He was feeling my energy and I knew it was even and balanced. Together we have had a powerful session in which the body dictated the experience at hand. The mind had contributed to the experience with its own visual imagery.

"How's the back feel?" Bruce checks in as I sit up on the massage table. I also know that Bruce has addressed what was most crucial in the moment. Even though the entry into the energy work was the lump on my back, the more critical work was with the energy block on my front side. It was for me to decipher any meaning to the dream image of the breast. For now, the most important work had been successfully completed.

"My back is sore but not nearly as sore as it was an hour ago. You have worked your magic again." I raise myself off the table and give Bruce a hug, very grateful for a masseuse who works with all that the body has to offer in the realm of imagery, energy, and Dreaming.

Chapter 8 Workout:

1. Identify your Dreaming practices. Do you desire to change them? Set your intent to do Dreaming today/tonight. Begin to Track your experiences. Recognize the difference between "dreaming" and "Dreaming". Identify dreams that you've had that signal both experiences.

2. "To be aware" is a function of the mind, whereas "awareness" is a perceptual act of the body—distinguish between the two by identifying an example from your own Dreaming.

3. Which of the examples of Dreaming appeals to you? How can you pursue that avenue of entering Dreaming?

4. Long to go into Dreaming. Look forward with every fiber of your being to accessing that state. Give your full attention to it!

5. What is your body's response to Dreaming?

9.
A Waste of Power

For the past week I'd been attending a workshop called Gateway at The Monroe Institute in West Virginia. Prompted to come by a desire to expand my consciousness, I experienced much that will take some time to unpack, sort-a-speak. All of the many things that occurred during the week, for others and for my self, indicated that there is available in the world much more than our eyes and ears take in. Truly the universe is an unfathomable mystery! My experience also corroborated my reading on the Toltec path. Indeed our perceptual abilities are underutilized, atrophied from nonuse. But they can be accessed and used differently than we've ever attempted to use them before and that's why I was here. What happened one morning was a prime example.

The program was designed around the use of HemiSync—the Monroe Institute's patented use of binaural beats layered underneath soothing music that when introduced to the brain effectively puts the listener into a meditative state. Much of the week was spent listening to tapes and CDs exploring the different states that can be achieved while the mind is in a "mind awake, body asleep" state. All week I'd been introduced to sounds, voices, images, memories, and experiences that had blown the lid off my very small world. Why, I had even channeled a male voice unfamiliar to me. Turns out another participant was waiting to hear from his deceased grandfather—and the grandfather spoke through me to get his grandson's attention; information was given that the grandson could readily identify as personal to him from his beloved grandfather.

I received information specific to me too, scary stuff that would take some time to unravel. How would the information effect changes in my life? Surely, it was time for dramatic change after hearing the brief conversation spoken by strangers. One morning lying in the CHEK unit, the single mattress enclosed in complete darkness used for listening to binaural beats, I heard two voices speaking. At first I was startled at hearing voices. Where had the voices come from since I was by myself in the CHEK unit? They were external to my vocal cords, not at all like the voice of Grandfather. Even after having heard voices and sounds, viewed images, and even felt a soft wind blowing inside the enclosed CHEK unit throughout the week, I was startled as it happened once again. The voices were not connected to any visual image that I could see.

"She's having trouble remembering," said the first voice. The second voice chuckled.

"No, the problem is she only remembers trouble." The voices faded.

Instantly, I knew what they were referring to—except that I had never looked at it from that perspective before. My heart pounded furiously. Monoliths of belief began to crumble. How could I have not remembered? How could I have forgotten something that seemed so obvious at that very moment? I was remembering the Other while at the same time I was recognizing the wasted time focused on remembering only troubles.

As a psychotherapist I spent far too much time focused on problems and woes and strife. I was immersed in my own and in those of others. Troubles were draining me.

It seems preposterous that once the warrior/sorcerer endeavors with such diligence to build her Power that she would carelessly do anything that would drain it from her. Alas, it happens and unfortunately, until the warrior/sorcerer recognizes that it happens, she may be in a "two steps forward, three steps back" situation. She may be so busy deciphering what builds and sustains Power that she misses wantonly, wasting what precious little she's come by at the same time. The good news is that there is a point in which Power itself takes charge and begins to plug up the drainage areas, allowing the warrior/sorcerer to tip that negative balance and build her Power base until a moment comes when Power is at her command.

A Waste of Power

Our first look will be at how Power can be drained from a hunter's point of view, then we'll look at common Power drains, and we'll end by discussing this most pernicious act called draining Power which can cripple the warrior/sorcerer in her development until she learns to master its wily ways.

The good news for the warrior/sorcerer is that she can only drain what she already possesses! Some readers may think this is only playing with semantics, but let's examine the word closely. "Draining" is the word being used here, but "leaking," "wasting," "misusing," or "depleting," can all be used interchangeably in context with Power. It is the act of taking something that we are already in possession of and rendering it ineffective. You cannot drain something you don't have! The warrior/sorcerer is in the position, if she is aware, to have Power to engage rather than to expend. Ah, the task of building Power has been in operation, and the warrior/sorcerer has been successful at the task that at first appeared to be so intangible! The task for the warrior/sorcerer is to find where and how the leak is occurring and to take action to stop it. At some point, the act of building Power supersedes the act of draining it. Recognizing when and where this happens is a critical maturation piece that will catapult the warrior/sorcerer into handling Power without wasting it.

Returning to the metaphor of the hunter and her prey, we want to focus on the manner in which the hunter conducts herself in order to be successful at the hunt. The hunter expends a critical amount of preparation before the hunt actually commences, and once the hunt is under way, she continues acting with stealth, purpose and patience. Unless she performs these preparatory actions she is simply out in the field waving a weapon in the air and, converse to her intentions, alerting every animal within miles of her foolishness. She is a wannabe warrior and hunter. But once she begins to act as though every move is of utmost importance and that her timing is critical to the operation of the hunt, then she truly enters into the dynamic exchange that has the potential for occurring. Even then subtle actions can determine prosperity or defeat.

Building on the Dreaming story at the beginning of this chapter shows how our awareness of an experience can be critical to either draining or building Power. Once the proverbial light bulb went on, and I recognized that my focus on troubles was blocking further movement I began to Track my thinking. I began to notice how often my mind would render as "a problem" any event that I either didn't like or didn't have an understanding of its significance or relevance to in my life. Further, I would then begin to "figure out" what to do about the "problem." The two mental actions (perceiving a problem and then figuring out what to do to resolve that problem) were endemic in my thinking. (Unfortunately, this is the Achilles' heal of many a therapist.) Seeing the pattern in my thinking as chronic was only a crack of an open door. I then needed to be able to continually Track and to alter that pattern. Tracking is the watchdog. It is the technique the hunter uses to locate the prey. At the moment of contact, the warrior/sorcerer needs to be active in taking down that thought pattern and/or changing the thought pattern to a different train of thought, or to a position of having no thought at all. Simply saying to myself, "There's that pattern again . . . I'm trying to figure out this problem," was a good starting point.

When the warrior/sorcerer begins to hunt down patterned thinking is exactly when she realizes how quickly the mind goes into action with a task that has been wrongly assigned it. Of course! The mind has been given a job that it fancies itself to be an expert at, but in actuality it has been assigned the task in error! The mind cannot conceive that "thinking" can occur in any other manner. The subtlety of the hunt would occur when my mind would defend its choice to problem solve—wasn't I acting as a psychotherapist, with clients that were paying me to assist them to problem solve? Didn't I need to address the problems in my marriage in an effort to resolve the stalemate between my husband and I? Beside, being a "problem solver" provided me with secondary gain. As a problem solver, I kept myself in business. As a problem solver, I kept myself busy feeling productive and clever at how astutely I could put a complex puzzle together. In other words, my "problem solving" fed my self-importance. With a mind so busy at putting together a thousand piece puzzle on an ongoing basis, there was little time to remember anything else, much less to remember the Other. If I entertained for one moment the choice of going into my mind's familiar pattern of "figuring out" I would often miss my target. My mind would be off and running doing what it had done as an occupation for years. Who wants to drop a behavior they fancy themselves to be good at performing? Under times of stress or hurry or apathy, I would fall into the patterned thinking by default, recognizing the pattern but falling for it anyway.

"Hey, there's that pothole in the middle of the street that I fell into yesterday—this time I'll avoid falling into it." I would stand and look at the pothole for a long time, congratulating myself on identifying where it stood in the middle of the road but failing to recognize that I was still as engaged with it as before. It took time to allow myself to go down another street entirely in order to never again fall into the gaping sinkhole in the asphalt, that hole that I'd fallen into hundreds and thousands of times as a matter of course. The subtlety was in not entertaining those thoughts on an ongoing basis, until due to non-use they phased away and atrophied, replaced by a quietness that didn't have any need to fix, or to problem solve, or to figure out. That's when the Other began to surface and make itself known. The prey had been captured.

In order to make this matter of recognizing Power drains very clear let's look at another example: talking. Yes—discussing, explaining, conversing, and dialoguing can be a colossal drain of Power. Even reading, a silent form of communicating can drain the warrior/sorcerer's Power! Yet, obviously we cannot avoid altogether what is unique to humans alone: communicating in spoken language.

How does the warrior/sorcerer distinguish between what is necessary communication and what is talking too much? Take a moment to consider whether or not you've ever spoken too much. Got that moment in your mind? Now Track who you were speaking with, what the topic of conversation revolved around, whether or not it had been the topic of conversation before, and whether or not you felt as though you had a choice to have the conversation from the beginning. The answers to those inquiries will inform you as to whether or not you've drained Power by talking. I remember talking when I wanted to impress, talking when I was bored, talking in defense, talking to persuade, talking to deceive. The goal is not necessarily to speak only the truth (doubtful whether that can happen anyway) or to only speak honestly, forthrightly, or directly. Those are expectations too easily loaded with morality. The goal is not to waste Power by talking too much. Only the individual warrior/sorcerer can determine for herself when and what that entails, what topics and words and subjects drain her Power.

There is another distinction to help the warrior/sorcerer determine whether she is talking too much and thereby squandering her Power. As the warrior/sorcerer begins to track her speech, she can also begin to pay attention to the level of attachment or detachment that is placed onto those words. We are more attached to our words when we have a hidden agenda that comes along with them. A story will help to flesh out this distinction, a story in which I was talking to myself—and, yes, even talking to oneself can evidence attachment or detachment.

One hot afternoon in Los Angeles I was driving the minivan belonging to the residential treatment home in which I was the social worker and therapist. I was thinking about my employment situation. I didn't like to work at the home. I was no good at working there. Therefore, I concluded that I was lousy at the job. As I drove along, cursing that the air conditioner didn't work and the minivan had turned into a mini oven, a fresh thought occurred to me. In the lull of driving in that hot van with my mind working a labyrinth of thought, I realized something big. I had erroneously connected two concepts that then lead to a further damaging conclusion. It went like this: because I didn't like working at a residential treatment home for adolescent girls, I was no good at working there. If I switched the two statements around it read differently: I was no good at working at the residential treatment home, therefore I didn't like working there. Which came first, the chicken or the egg? In the end it didn't much matter. What was important to notice was that I had wedded the two concepts. I was not effective at working as the social worker and therapist for those adolescent girls therefore I was lousy at the job.

In addition, I had added an erroneous conclusion: I should make myself do a better job! Those girls needed the support and resources that a social worker and therapist had to give. In other words, I had added ethics and morality into the mix. I was attached to an arbitrary, yet damaging, definition of what I should be doing! What kept me from coming to the conclusion that I didn't like the job therefore I would find another one? What kept me attached to a train of thought, a virtual "talking head," that had drained my Power so effectively? My agenda had been to force myself to stay in a position regardless of the fit between the job site and me. Once looked at from this perspective it came dangerously close to a saying told to me over and over as a child, "You make your bed, you lie in it." Damaging and draining talk, indeed!

Beyond the examples already given, common means of draining Power are legion. They are also entirely unique to the warrior/sorcerer and where they may be on the Toltec path. Draining Power can happen on the physical, mental, spiritual, or energetic level, as an exchange between people, places, things, or while Tracking or Dreaming. Draining Power can happen consciously or in an unaware state. For the mind to be aware of what is happening is not a prerequisite for draining or building Power! Not at all—and this may initially be a surprise to the warrior/sorcerer. Yet draining Power can happen only for as long as the warrior/sorcerer lacks the awareness that allows her to act differently, in addition to the volition to change her actions. Depending on the bent of every individual warrior/sorcerer the drain of Power can be more treacherous in certain areas, while other areas may be easy to curtail. The warrior/sorcerer experiences both: the easy Power drains that are plugged up upon first becoming aware of them, and the more difficult Power drains that are part and parcel of who we think we are, to such an extent that we don't even recognize we're losing anything. Then there are those Power drains that come at the beginning of our journey and those that come as we advance further down the path. Draining Power comes at every turn of the road even though the mask it can wear changes endlessly.

Draining Power can be as nebulous as sustaining Power. Not surprisingly there are many Power drains found in the psychological

Encounter with Power

matrix, in the world of how we relate to ourselves and to others. Once we recognize them they are easier to walk away from, but they can be buried in our socialization and therefore take some uprooting in order to call them to task. There are two means of draining Power that I want to discuss more fully. They are subtle and yet are a pervasive part of our socialization or the manner in which we are all raised in the human milieu.

The first one I call "wanting, wishing, and hoping." Years ago a common vernacular used in the mental health field for these three words were, "woulda, coulda, shoulda". The mindset these three words puts the average person into is a passive one—if only things were different; if only she'd done something besides what she actually did; if only the future would hold more than the present moment! The mindset robs the warrior/sorcerer of her Power and drains her from taking action. She runs the risk of living life in the past or in the future rather than in the present moment. There are many on a Toltec path that will quickly point out that there is only the present moment; there is no past and no future. I agree with them. The "past" and "future" I'm speaking of are a construct of the mind and have no vitality at all from a warrior/sorcerer's point of view. But these are constructs of the mind that are endemic to our social upbringing and are subtle in their influence. They are constructs that at first blush seem to be harmless and to engender positive motivation for action. If seen from a different point of view, a warrior/sorcerer's point of view, they do exactly the opposite. They paralyze and prevent any action from taking place at all. To be challenged to give up wanting and wishing and hoping evokes argument because these three are wolves in sheep's clothing. They've been dressed as sheep for so long they aren't easily recognized.

When I first began reading about the Toltec path it was through the books of Carlos Castaneda, however, I began reading them twenty some years after most folks my age. Somewhere in my slumber during the years in which Castaneda was alive and still writing, I didn't have a conscious clue about the sorcery world. When I did begin reading Castaneda, and talking with others about what I was reading, people would comment,

"Oh, him? I read him in college." End of discussion. He was apparently from bygone days and of little relevance to a middle-aged adult picking his books up for the first time. Sound like living in the "past"? That didn't deter me, however, and I continued to read. In fact, I began to read the books for a second and third time. Something in them captured a part of me that had been dormant and I wanted more. This one's a giveaway: wanting.

I ventured into the unknown and began to experiment with some of the things Castaneda wrote about. If I could only have some of those same experiences! Now you're onto it: wishing. For some time, I practiced the things he wrote about—and wished with a strangling intensity that my experiences would match his. I began to look for ways to duplicate how to experience what he did—and things started happening! Strange things began to happen that I didn't understand and couldn't explain. My hope was fervent and endless: "When, oh when, was my Don Juan going to show up?" Hoping for further instruction, I moved into close proximity to someone who might be able to tell me what was happening and to teach me the way. The mood that always placed attainment, just out of reach and dangling like a carrot in front of my nose, was hope, the last of the wicked stepsisters! These three constructs of the mind kept me busy for quite a period of time trying to figure out what I was doing wrong and lamenting that Castaneda must have been either mistaken about the sorcery path (i.e. a liar), or the only one able to practice (i.e. a guru.) By continually lapsing into moods that had nothing to do with, and run counter to, walking with Power, I was continually draining what little Power I had.

Now for one more colossal drain on Power. It is sandwiched in amongst the last few sentences above. It will clip a warrior/sorcerer's wings and keep her from ever flying free if it is not recognized and dealt with. It is subtle and pervasive in a society that delineates between two types of people: leaders and followers. The fallacy of the belief even permeates Toltec crowds. It will drain Power through and through until the warrior/sorcerer no longer recognizes their inheritance within the very heart of Power itself. The belief is this: the student needs a teacher.

Encounter with Power

Long did I believe that I could not walk the Toltec path without becoming the apprentice or student of someone who traveled the path before I had arrived. This assumption is rampant in esoteric literature. "When the student is ready the teacher will appear." My assumption was to expect two things: number one, the teacher would be a human being, and number two, the student and the teacher were not the same person. Both of these assumptions can be grossly erroneous. In fact, they can be dead wrong in the light of the Other.

The first assumption came from my expectations. If I was going to pursue this path, then I needed someone to teach me. And, if I was to find a teacher, it needed to be someone who had the credentials to do the job. Not faulty reasoning—but, neither is it from a sorcery perspective. Let me be frank: this thought process comes blatantly from the books of Carlos Castaneda and other Toltec authors. And, due to Castaneda's ground breaking knowledge of what sorcery is about via his books, there comes too easily an unspoken agreement that all he wrote is accurate and true to this path for anyone else who is pursuing it. This thought process also comes blatantly from Western thought. Our entire educational system is built on the paradigm of the pair, student and teacher. The assumption is not always a safe one to make. A teacher is vital, beneficial, and relevant to becoming a warrior/sorcerer, but a teacher is not always another human being. Wanting, wishing, and hoping for another human being to be our teacher can drain our Power.

I have been taught by the wind, by the trail, and by the birds flying overhead. Books have taught me; the fire has taught me, as have caves. I have been taught by dreams, by Dreaming, and by omens. I have been taught by four-footed creatures, by trees, and by cars on the freeway. I have been taught by intuition, by moods, and by color. The sources that have taught me are numerous—and, I didn't always honor them as such because I was too busy looking and waiting for my teacher to appear. In this, I am not too unusual. I have seen with my eyes, ears, and heart, how many people want to give their Power to a teacher, to a workshop leader, to a guru, or to another sorcerer.

The second error that is easy to make regarding a teacher, is that the teacher will be outside of the warrior/sorcerer, in other words, the teacher will be extant to who the warrior/sorcerer is. This thinking error is even more slippery than the first assumption that the teacher must be human. "Okay, I can agree that an outside agent can be a teacher to me, but what exactly are you saying here?" I am saying that YOU can be a teacher to yourself. We want to define carefully who the "you" is, but I am saying a warrior/sorcerer can be a teacher to his or her self. This is the Other. This is energy developed to such an extent by the warrior/sorcerer that they evolve themselves beyond their humanity. It is possible and it is desirable. But it takes getting outside of the thinking error that says that someone outside of us is better up to the task than we are.

When we are able to ask ourselves the following question and to answer it affirmatively we are on our way to becoming wholly responsible for who and what we are in the sorcery realm. "Am I capable and willing to teach myself?" When we answer with a resounding "Yes!" then the mystery really begins because it is the Other who is our teacher, that mysterious being who comes into creation from the Power within each warrior/sorcerer. That is when we begin to invest in the Power we do have rather than to drain it uselessly. This Other that has been mentioned here and there but not fully explained needs a separate volume of work. For now, know that as the warrior/sorcerer works with the experiences that can be had from acting on the techniques throughout this book, the Other is silently and quietly gaining enough Power to consolidate and introduce herself as though Power has taken form from out of the void.

How to explain an employment position I had waited nine months for— as though it was a crowning achievement of a live birth? It appeared as though major events happened for me within this human gestation period and this time was no exception. I left a position in Human Services and walked into a position within the Department of Education with this odd nine-month gap in between. The experience was one of initially draining Power, but then went through a strange metamorphosis into one of Power plugging up holes in the end. I'd never seen anything like it!

Encounter with Power

After careful deliberation and timing that was an earmark of sorceric events, I was at home without the full-time position that had drained me energetically and emotionally for a couple of years. My plan was to write while I waited for a new position to open itself up. And the new position would come—without a doubt! I had stood in the middle of a neighborhood street in the early morning light of a fine spring day and had commanded Power to bring a new position which would allow me to follow my calling, while also allowing me to make a living and pay bills. The months crept along—interviews came and went—and still no job opportunity came that would fit my specifications. Six months into "no job" and it was beginning to look much more like "no money." Maybe those offers I had turned down had been a mistake to not take. Maybe I was asking for too much—to make a living but to also have the wherewithal to do my writing. My old pernicious habit of worrying reared its ugly head—where was the job I had called to me? How much longer could I live on savings? What happened to the Power I had commanded in the middle of the Makiki neighborhood? Face to face with worry and it didn't take long to see how quickly and viciously worry eats away at this warrior/sorcerer's Power! At nine months on the dot, a new position arrived.

But then an odd turnabout took place! How could a job be too good to be true? My new position was a site coordinator position for a program within the Department of Education. The program had been highly funded but strangely underutilized. I was the program coordinator for an educational program with four staff and two kids! Our capacity was for an enrollment of eight to ten, but not once in my first year in the program did we have over three to four kids on the enrollment at any given time, and never more than two kids in the classroom. Talk about lots of free time! I was not expected to fill an enrollment quota. It was only expected that I would handle the daily operations within school hours of a program with two students. Needless to say, I had time to write!

What I didn't expect to have happen was to have this sense of guilt that I was not doing my job fully because I had afternoons practically free! Power stepped in! In an uncanny way I began to notice a strange turn of events. Whenever people stopped by (translated: supervisors or district personnel) I would be actively performing my job responsibilities. Whenever the phone would ring, I would be available to answer and respond to the request. Whenever staff was absent another would step up and perform the necessary job, freeing me up as a result. Whenever I was called forth to perform in any way, I was available and willing to respond! All of this, and I continued to have several hours per day to sit in front of a computer and write! Power bulldozed through angst at the first position and unwarranted guilt (is guilt ever really warranted anyway?) at the second position to see to it that I was able to fulfill the task that was my calling. Power had plugged up any drainage and supplied me with both income and time to do those things that were closest and dearest to my heart.

Chapter 9 Workout:

1. In what ways do you waste or drain your Power?

2. Draining Power can easily occur due to how we've been socialized. Identify a Power drain that is perpetuated for you due to societal pressure. Examples are: climbing the corporate ladder, materialism, political maneuvering, and relationship expectations. Identify your social Power drain. What can you do to lessen that energy expenditure?

3. "Wanting, wishing, and hoping" can keep us living perpetually in the past or forever in the future. If this is a Power drain for you, what can you do to change this pattern of thinking and acting?

4. How have you given over your growth/maturation/learning/education to someone outside of yourself?

5. Are you capable and willing to teach yourself? This does not mean never again gaining knowledge from an extant teacher, becoming an apprentice or student of another, or reading of other's knowledge via the written word. It does mean that at some point in time you will be capable of being your own teacher. Is that time now?

10.
Tale of Power

Every warrior/sorcerer has a tale of Power. We go through these experiences and whether we recognize them as tales of Power or not are entirely up to each one of us. It is not any different than when we first recognize Power and then begin to engage with it as only a warrior/sorcerer can after acknowledging its relevance to our lives. At first, Power was far-fetched and even foreign—an odd experience to encounter that promises to supply us with the energy we need on this path. Then Power became not only vital to our growth and sustenance but we found it to be indispensable, something we could not do without. Tales of Power are much the same. Initially, they are easily overlooked because they are not recognized for what they truly are. Eventually they become the pulse of where we are on the path, and we would no more do without them than to go without food for nourishment or air to breathe.

Experience can become the sine qua non or a "must have" as we develop and mature as warrior/sorcerers. It is easy to come to expect that in order to develop we must have experience—and this is largely accurate. The point here is to shift the focus of attention off of experience and place it squarely onto the bull's eye: Power is the mediating force of experience and is therefore the aim, not the experience itself. This is a subtle shift but a critical one for the warrior/sorcerer to be aware of. Power is the very lifeblood of the warrior/sorcerer. Without it we perish.

How then does someone else's tale of Power impact if our goal is to have our own and to take it in as the very lifeblood that it is? What does a tale of Power do for the warrior/sorcerer? What does reading collective warrior/sorcerer's tales of Power do for the individual warrior/sorcerer? We are social beings, even as warrior/sorcerers, and hearing and reading tales of Power serve to instruct, admonish, guide, challenge, motivate, and encourage every warrior/sorcerer at the precise spot they happen to be at when the tale is heard. In this last chapter we will look at a tale of Power—a collection of stories during the length of one year—that involves every single subject covered in this book. See whether or not you can site the subjects as they occur in the life of one warrior/sorcerer on her trek to freedom. Power weaves itself into the very matrix of the warrior/sorcerer and how it unveils itself is as individual as a snowflake. What will come through is the pulsing, throbbing, beating of Power itself as it impacts a life and challenges the warrior/sorcerer to reach beyond what she believes herself capable of and thrusts her into the unknown. For the warrior/sorcerer the unknown is exactly where she wants to be.

March 29

It was the second day in our new place and I arose early to walk the half-mile to the neighborhood coffee shop. Buying a latte and a scone fresh out of the oven, I sat for a few minutes enjoying my breakfast. The dream earlier that morning arose in my memory together with the aroma of blueberry on the dish in front of me. "Listen—feel—speak" Hmm, there was much more to the sentence when I first heard it, but I lay in bed without moving, not wanting to get up and write it down. "I'll remember," I told myself, but I didn't remember. Those three words were the only ones left by the time I got out of bed.

A woman entered my room and approached me. Gliding noiselessly over to the bed she lowered her lips to my left ear and spoke softly. I had lain as though paralyzed, transfixed at my bedroom door being opened by someone who didn't live in the house, and that I hadn't known was even there. I lay there kicking myself for not getting up and writing the complete sentence down. No matter, I would pay attention to the words that stayed with me. Getting up from the small table I placed my empty cup and saucer onto the countertop and left the little café. It was time to go home and get on the computer.

Glancing around at the neighborhood while walking I marveled that we had found a place to rent in town. "So close to the coffee shop," I mused. Escrow on the sell of my place in California would close in a month in order for me to buy a home in Hawaii, but for now this six month rental would suit our needs perfectly. My thoughts rambled aimlessly as they were wont to do while walking and soon they wandered into my place of employment. "How much longer can I work with these kids?" It was the question of the hour. Six months ago, I agreed to work as the therapist for a temporary time, until a position in the large non-profit agency could be created for me at the management level. For months now, I had been working at two residential homes, one for girls and one for boys: children removed from their homes for sundry reasons. These kids were a tough crowd to work with, particularly when a cloud of turmoil, crisis, and confrontation hung over them most of the time. Years ago I had stopped working with the same population due to a lack of desire and fit for the job. Despite their need and my initial direction to work with them given my reservations, time was running out. I was drained and the agency was set on "full throttle", doing what an agency does for a challenging population. The turmoil, crisis, and confrontation wouldn't end any time soon.

Suddenly, a thought without any emotion attached to it popped into my head, "Command Power to bring you a new job." It was as clear as the ocean view to my left on this paradise island. Without hesitation, I put the thought into a command, "It's time for a new job—a job that will allow me to write, a job that won't squeeze me dry. Bring it to me." I was clear, confident, and in command. Following the bidding of the woman's voice that whispered in my ear earlier that morning, I commanded Power to act on my behalf.

April 19

"Mom, I had a dream. It's for you." My daughter's voice sounded urgent over the phone, not from having had the dream because that was not uncommon, but from something else I couldn't read in her voice.

"I awoke from the dream because it was a nightmare. I haven't had a nightmare in a long time. Here it is." She launched into the dream without taking another breath. I quickly grabbed a pen and paper to write the dream down.

"I knew that monks were going to torture you; you accepted that it was going to happen. I looked in the refrigerator and saw your limbs in plastic containers. You wanted to share your limbs with the agency you work for."

'But it's too much meat!' I cried aloud. I began to yell until I saw you lying in bed. A bright light radiated throughout the entire room. The monks were lined around the bed; they were keeping watch. I felt no evil intent from them. I was terribly sad, like I was at a funeral. Surgery had removed your arms and legs even though I could see all of the organs in your body as though your skin was translucent. The stitches were fine and precise, exquisite in fact. I was overwhelmed with sadness. You said, 'Oh, Carla— I almost let myself feel the pain at my plight—but I didn't—I made it through.' Mom, I awoke from the dream, I was so upset. It was like I awoke from a nightmare. What do you think the dream is about?"

I shared the plight with my daughter. The agency work was draining me even though I was convinced that the job had been handed to me upon my arrival in Hawaii by the very forces that had moved me to come in the first place. After nearly two years of trying, I had finally admitted to myself that I could no longer work at the position and follow my path with heart at the same time. I simply didn't have the time or energy to do both with any effectiveness. My direct supervisor, Lima, was a workhorse and sixty-some hour weeks were not unusual. The dream was telling me that I had given enough; there was no longer a need for me to try and do what I could no longer do. The dream had come through her because I was having a difficult time letting go, even though I was burned out—how in the world would I get another position to support me financially that would allow me to do what I most wanted and it not be a position that was simply trading apples for apples—another non-profit agency position that would expect more than I had to give?

April 24

The annual meeting for Puuhale was held in the morning. It was an all staff mandatory meeting. That's not usually a good sign— to be ordered to a meeting. The CEO rose at the end of the day and spoke for forty-five minutes about the agency's position within the state of Hawaii. With the current decisions being made at the state level, the agency's viability was on rocky ground. His message was full of pessimism and doom. I drove home downcast.

Pulling into the driveway, I opened the car door slowly. Space is so tight in Hawaii! Our driveway is large enough for the size of a small compact. "But I'm driving a small compact and it's still a tight squeeze," I mutter. The meeting hung over me like a thundercloud.

With sudden movement a creature flies into my face. It is so near my eyes I can't make out what it is. Swerving, I duck down as it flies at me again. Then the creature flutters to the top of the carport. It is a large white and gray black moth with a wingspan of nearly four inches. The same type moth I'd seen in the bathroom before joining a group meditation months ago. It was here again! I look at the moth now lying completely still on the ceiling with its wings spread like an open book. Instantly,

I know it is an omen. "What are you here for?" I ask. "It is about Puuhale. Don't despair. The situation will take care of itself in four months time."

April 27

I'm tired, exhausted really. As I enter the national forestry trail sandwiched at the end of the old houses in the midst of busy Makiki, I pause. "What am I so tired from?" Putting any question to the trail always nets a response. The trail has become my confidante and mentor—guiding and instructing when my mind and heart are muddled and weary. I come regularly, listening for Spirit when everywhere else the world is spinning too fast. My tennis shoes place themselves one after the other in steady rhythm as I climb the trail, but my mind is still. "Your defensiveness makes you tired. Historically the way you respond when someone evaluates you has not been positive. Separate their energy from your own; separate their expectations from your own. When you buy into them you defend." My conversation yesterday with the program director came back to me.

"From where I sit, certain people, who are strong and talented, aren't placed in the most effective positions to take full advantage of their strengths." Lima looked directly at me as she twirled the ring on her finger, a habit she had when she held a firm opinion. I had approached Lima about her earlier promise, a promise that appeared to be slipping increasingly into the future.

"If I was given the authority, I would place them where they might be better utilized. But recently my decision making power—and this is just between us—has been taken from me. The time to move may not be now. We may need to wait a while longer." Lima never spoke in a straight line from point A to B, although if you listened long enough her meaning was as direct as an arrow hitting bull's eye. Another forty-five minutes of discussing the all staff meeting and the CEO's lack of motivational style two days before brought her around again to the reason for our discussion.

"Tell me how you would envision the Assistant Director Position?" She spoke of the position promised months earlier if only I would fill in at the two residential homes for a short while.

"It may be that the greatest need is for you to stay where you are. Your strengths may be best used there. In fact, can you watch over the programs while I go on vacation for the month of June?"

The month of June was within the four-month time period foretold by the gray moth. But my loyalties were divided; Lima expected more than I wanted to give and I wanted more than she had to give. This growing schism between us, where once there was none, was about time and commitment and expectations and even sacrifice. Lima was asking for something I'd already given—didn't she see that?

May 5

The staff meeting was over and the room was emptied of people within a few minutes, leaving Lima and me standing facing each other. I smiled in nervous anticipation.

"Lima, I'm giving my notice to leave Puuhale after you return from your vacation. I wanted to tell you now rather than when you come back in July. It'll give you plenty of time to find someone to fill my position." Lima fingered her ring unconsciously. I watched as she spoke slowly but directly in a way I'd not heard before.

"What I intended for you to hear when we last spoke was that if you move into the Assistant Director position you would be faced with what I've been faced with for the past five years, an agency that will suck you dry. I've been telling the CEO that you were going to quit—we can't keep placing responsibility onto you that isn't yours to shoulder."

She was referring to the decision made a month ago in which I became responsible for the medication monitoring in the program, a duty the registered nurse used to fill. Suddenly, I'd become the liaison between the psychiatrist and the clients and was responsible to track all of the prescription medications for ten heavily medicated youths. One misstep and the agency would be cited in violation of state regulations.

My decision to give notice, based on a BSK, a boys scout knife, had come to me while hiking earlier that morning. At the end of the trail and a long conversation about my position with Puuhale, I looked down and found a red BSK —an omen loud and clear. "Be prepared to cut out a significant portion of your life today!" I followed the direction the omen pointed. Omens had never led me astray, but always one step ahead of where I might otherwise lead myself without them.

May 16

Duality—the word kept coming back to me again and again. I must pay attention. I saw the movie "X-men" last night, a movie about the duality of human-looking beings, which are really mutants with extraordinary abilities that end up at war with regular human beings. Right now, I'm at war with the duality of appearance and how one event can be viewed from two such different perspectives.

How am I viewing my time with Puuhale? There is duality occurring. The warrior/sorcerer's conviction that a silent force is moving and directing their actions is evident. But from a daily perspective it looks as though I am moralizing my position: "Puuhale won't give me what I want and therefore I'm outta here!" Just because the time frame had shifted didn't mean I had to take a stand against them. Yet, I knew that morality has no weight in the Toltec world, much as we may think that it does. Actions are not generated by morality, good vs. bad, or right vs. wrong. Acts have Power. The Power in the acts is not determined by their "goodness" or "badness," by their efficacy as determined by my value system. Acts either increase or decrease my energy.

I have been interpreting my actions through the lens of a worldview and not from a warrior/sorcerer's view. I am mutant but treating myself as human. I smiled at the analogy. It fit my circumstances. When I am able to live each moment fully, there will be no duality. The majority of humans live in a world of duality—human meaning that we relegate to a natural law just as we do the concept of time. There is no duality for those with a worldview large enough to see the whole.

May 21

I do not know what to do about a job. Call about the interview I had last week? Do I call and withdraw the résumé I sent to the same agency where I'd interviewed two years earlier? They'd offered me a position two years ago but I turned it down due to the awkward feeling in that place. Would I simply be trading one chaos-ridden milieu for another? How in the world am I going to get out of the human service field with a position that can support me financially? Did I really command Power to bring me a new position that day I walked home from the coffee shop two months ago? How long will it take? I had put out enough résumés to get a bite— like bait on a hook someone would respond. "But Hawaii is not in a hurry," I reminded myself.

Driving all the way to the west end of the island this morning, I gazed out at the ocean. The drive was forty-five minutes across a sixty-mile wide island, nearly all the way across, but I had never minded driving in a car. Always I would go into a state of ease and higher awareness, highway hypnosis for sure. Gazing out at the early morning sun glistening on the ocean blue, I pondered what to do.

"Sea, as far as the eye can see." The expanse was endless and my eye traveled all the way to where the ocean and the sky conjoined.

"See, as far as the 'I' can see." Take action on what I see—I don't want another agency position. On most days I am clear about that.

"See, as far as the eye can see." Trust I am seeing clearly and not merely looking on a surface level. As much as I'm able to—take action. Take one day at a time and do exactly what needs to be done for that day; tomorrow will take care of itself.

I pulled into the driveway at the girl's program. The higher awareness continued: I am tripped up on what I need to be doing, and on the expectation that I should be able to see farther ahead of me than I really can in order to know what steps to take. Yes, I commanded Power, but that means Power will move on my behalf rather than, or at least instead of, the "I" that loves to figure everything out goes into action. The site manager came out of the house as I approached the front door.

"We've had some trouble with medications this morning," *she said with a serious tone. I sighed. It was going to be a long day.*

I had commanded Power two months ago, but at this very moment I was tired and low in energy and without a warrior/sorcerer's purpose.

May 26

Walking to my car after my early morning hike, I reached for the keys in the pocket of my shorts. The car key fit uneasily into the lock.

"Unusual for it not to slide in smoothly," *I thought absentmindedly. I opened the glove compartment to take out my wallet. No wallet to be found! Immediately I glanced around as though the thief would be hiding around the closest tree or bush watching me discover the dirty deed. I felt exposed, as though a voyeur had been watching me and knew where I lived. By the time I drove the ten minutes it took me to get to a phone and call to cancel my credit cards one of them had already been used at a Fast Gas.*

"Geez, they don't waste time," *I moaned,* "of all times not to be carrying a cell phone."

My interview with Concern for Children didn't go well last week. Seated in a new red suit answering the typical interview questions, I had a funny feeling. This job wasn't for me—sure, I would be traveling between islands on an as needed basis, and that could be fun, but at what cost? The job was based on agency compliance with state regulations. That translated into being on the front line with agency noncompliance and being the mediator between errant agency personnel and state auditors looking at the letter of the law. My red suit was the picture of duality: my favorite color that usually swung any interview to my advantage and at the same time the color that screams, "Stop!" *Did I blow the interview or was the position not for me?*

Funny—when I have Power, opportunities open up that don't open up otherwise, and when I feel powerless, I feel depleted. I feel as empty as a gas tank with no fuel on a barren desert road. That suit was simply the road sign to that job. The stolen wallet? I had no self-pity about being robbed, but neither did I have enough Power to keep it from happening.

June 4

"Lima will be leaving upon her return from her vacation," Celie spoke in almost a whisper. "Keep it under wraps until next week. What are your plans? Would you consider staying for awhile until things settle down?" Celie was Lima's friend and fellow program director. By her questions I knew Lima had told her about my notice to quit before she'd left the week before.

"I'm not set on any specific date to leave. I'll be here through this month, then let's talk again," I assured her. Could I be any more confused about what was happening? Meanwhile, I had spoken to a real estate agent and mortgage broker about buying in Hawaii. There was not much possibility of getting a mortgage loan if I had a brand new job—loan companies wanted job longevity, not job-hopping—two years was their rule of thumb for place of employment, and I was shy of the two-year mark by a few months. I had begun looking for something to buy, amidst going to job interviews, making sure all the clients were taking their medications on schedule, and filling in for Lima. Could I possibly find a new job amongst everything else I was doing within the same month?

June 21

My perspective was beginning to alter. If I can make it through this time of low morale and constant busyness with Lima away, then possibly my position at Puuhale can be redesigned after all. The thought of going to another agency with similar dynamics seemed totally pointless.

For the past two weeks, strange events had occurred. I made an offer on one house only to withdraw the offer a week later. A day later and the first place I had looked at two months previous came back on the market after falling out of escrow—and, I had a second offer in the works. But look at this dream from last night—a strange one in light of entertaining the idea of staying at Puuhale. "Nothing is as clear as I'd like it to be," I reminded myself. This is the condition of the warrior/sorcerer, isn't it? The unknown can bring such a sense of uncertainty that I immediately want to define and clarify what is happening around me so that I can gain something known. If I can only hold onto my sense that Power will find a way and not let confusion reign.

In the dream I was standing at the foot of a stairway with a baby in a stroller. The baby wanted the raw hamburger plainly visible on the last step of the staircase, but as I approached the step to pick it up, I saw a cougar, facing away from me, eating the hamburger. Stealthily and slowly, I edged the stroller out of the doorway and pulled the door closed to remove myself from any danger. Staring at the latch on the door, I watched it close, moving in exaggerated slowness. Once the door was closed, I knew we would be out of danger.

The meaning of the dream didn't take long in coming. It was as though it came by way of megaphone: "The door to Puuhale is closing! Don't pull back and remain on the other side of the door away from the staircase and the cougar! The cougar is Power! The staircase will lead up and away from your current situation. Keep yourself on the side of the door that leads upstairs. Don't let your apprehension remove you from your source of energy and sustenance."

June 30

Celie looked uncomfortable as I entered her office and sat down. She had called and asked that I drop by before heading out for the programs on the other side of the island. I had recently requested to take all of my paid time off—nearly a month's worth—as soon as Lima returned from her vacation. No new job was in site, but the time off would allow me to step away from Puuhale for a short time and allow for my escrow to close before I actually gave a date to leave.

"I have bad news," Celie didn't beat around the bush, almost the polar opposite of the way in which Lima handled interactions.

"John won't sign off on your hours. He heard from your site managers that you were leaving and so he wants you to give an end date for your employment. Did you tell them you were leaving?" I sighed.

"Better not to go into any detective or lab work in which precision counts," I thought wryly. I had indeed mentioned to them that I was thinking about leaving. I had never imagined that my plaintive admission on a semi-private basis in an agency with over two hundred employees would get back to the CEO in a week's time. I sighed again and told Celie what I'd said.

"Okay, here's how you do it." Celie explained how to arrange partial time off with no difficulty in getting it signed off, return to work for two weeks, give a two week notice, and walk away with the additional hours owed. I didn't mention to her (lesson learned!) that after those specified weeks, my escrow would be closing at the same time. Arranging my time according to her recommendations would ensure that I would be employed through the close of the escrow.

March 1

Today I started my new job! For months I had remained home and like a chrysalis in a cocoon, transformed into something I scarcely imagined I could become while working. Left to my own devices I would have remained at Puuhale, making do in the situation; fear had almost gotten the better of me. But Power stepped in and blasted my uncertainty by forcing me to be accountable. That "leak" of information to the site managers had placed me in the position to give a date to leave the agency. Why is it that as human beings we often need to push ourselves beyond our comfort zone to actually grow and to evolve?

The fall and winter months were not easy—day in and day out wondering what was going to happen. Where were Power and the new job I'd commanded? I learned that time is a daily commodity we think we have, whereas timing is of the Other. I learned that a paycheck doesn't determine the well being of a warrior/sorcerer. I learned that the state of well being that I am in is more important than the job or career that I attend to. I learned that once commanded, Power doesn't back down as I so often felt like doing. I learned that Power is Power regardless of any circumstances—its energy doesn't vacillate according to outward events or inward mood. I learned that Power provides even when everything looks dismal and dark. And, I *learned that Power is the only fuel source that will supply the warrior/sorcerer throughout her journey.*

The task of looking at Power through a magnifying glass is at an end. It has been a journey filled with the intent of one warrior/sorcerer convinced that taking a closer look at this abstract force would be of benefit to anyone reading along. Before we end, however, there is one last concept that involves Power that has not yet been mentioned: saving of the best for last, perhaps. Of course, it comes through a tale of Power.

I was hiking a jungle trail while pondering a subject matter that would capture my attention and focus on what to write about. A dozen ideas were swirling around inside my head. They were ideas that I had mulled over for too long. It was time to get started and to quit pondering. Enough already of my thinking and evaluating and obsessing about a topic that might capture the attention of an audience! It was time to act. It was time to seat myself down at the computer and write. I became acutely aware that as I sloshed through the mucky, rain sodden trail that the moment had arrived. There—on the trail—the topic to write about would manifest, not tomorrow, or next week after more thought, or in six months when I was further along in my warrior/sorcerer training. But at that very moment the decision would be born.

I put the question to the trail, "At this moment in my life what is the topic for me to write about?" I stood stock-still. With every fiber of my being, I knew that whatever came into my still and quiet mind would be what I would write about. Power is decisive! Power does not vacillate due to indecision and a feeling of inadequacy. Power acts!

"Power is the third enemy of the warrior/sorcerer—the being who is on her journey to freedom. Write about Power as an enemy." Spirit spoke clearly. The challenge has been to do that very thing from the moment of standing under the canopy of Hawaiian flora to this very moment seated in front of my laptop. Questions have sprouted up like dandelions on a spring lawn but I have continued to take action. If given free reign, the questions would have become continual barriers to my progress. If I stopped for a moment, I would have lost the battle.

Encounter with Power

Writing this book has been my battle with Power. What Power did that day was to set up a doorway, a portal, an entryway, and offered for me to step through it. A premise was set up for me to act upon. The premise was that I had enough knowledge of Power to be a spokeswoman for it. Not that it needed one—but Power is mysterious enough to use a warrior/sorcerer to suit its purposes. Power will do the same for any warrior/sorcerer with enough personal power to pay attention. Power challenges us to do what we think we cannot do, and then provides us with all that we need to accomplish the task! Challenge Power today and find out for yourself that Power is the rightful inheritance of the warrior/sorcerer traveling the road to freedom! Experience Power in all of its manifestations, unique to who you are with all of your permutations and foibles, strengths and weaknesses, and you will discover that you have your own tale of Power to share.

Chapter 10 Workout:

1. Identify a time when you were clear, confident, and in command. This is Power!

2. When have you commanded Power to act on your behalf?

3. Where do you go to hear Power speak to you? Find a place that will allow you to listen and to hear what Power has to say.

4. What doorway has Power set up for you to walk through?

5. What is your tale of Power?

6. Who do you want to hear your tale? Tell them. There is Power in telling a tale!

To contact the author email at: eyeonenlightenment@gmail.com

Made in the USA
Middletown, DE
07 January 2022